Learning to Work

D1059131

Brookings Dialogues on Public Policy

The presentations and discussions at Brookings conferences and seminars often deserve wide circulation as contributions to public understanding of issues of national importance. The Brookings Dialogues on Public Policy series is intended to make such papers and commentary available to a broad and general audience. The series supplements the Institution's research publications by reflecting the contrasting, often lively, and sometimes conflicting views of elected and appointed government officials, other leaders in public and private life, and scholars. In keeping with their origin and purpose, the Dialogues are not subjected to the same formal review procedures established for the Institution's research publications. Brookings publishes the contributions to the Dialogues in the belief that they are worthy of public consideration but does not assume responsibility for their objectivity and for the accuracy of every factual statement. And, as in all Brookings publications, the judgments, conclusions, and recommendations presented in the Dialogues should not be ascribed to the trustees, officers, or other staff members of the Brookings Institution.

Learning to Work
Employer Involvement in School-to-Work Transition Programs

Edited by

THOMAS R. BAILEY

THE BROOKINGS INSTITUTION / Washington, D.C.

Copyright © 1995 by
THE BROOKINGS INSTITUTION
1775 Massachusetts Avenue, N.W.
Washington, D.C. 20036

LIBRARY OF CONGRESS CATALOG CARD NUMBER 95-077616
ISBN 0-8157-0773-8

9 8 7 6 5 4 3 2 1

₿ THE BROOKINGS INSTITUTION

The Brookings Institution is an independent organization devoted to nonpartisan research, education, and publication in economics, government, foreign policy, and the social sciences generally. Its principal purposes are to aid in the development of sound public policies and to promote public understanding of issues of national importance.

The Institution was founded on December 8, 1927, to merge the activities of the Institute for Government Research, founded in 1916, the Institute of Economics, founded in 1922, and the Robert Brookings Graduate School of Economics and Government, founded in 1924.

The Board of Trustees is responsible for the general administration of the Institution, while the immediate direction of the policies, program, and staff is vested in the President, assisted by an advisory committee of the officers and staff. The by-laws of the Institution state: "It is the function of the Trustees to make possible the conduct of scientific research, and publication, under the most favorable conditions, and to safeguard the independence of the research staff in pursuit of their studies and in the publication of the result of such studies. It is not a part of their function to determine, control, or influence the conduct of particular investigations or the conclusions reached."

The President bears final responsibility for the decision to publish a manuscript as a Brookings book. In reaching his judgment on competence, accuracy, and objectivity of each study, the President is advised by the director of the appropriate research program and weighs the views of a panel of expert outside readers who report to him in confidence on the quality of the work. Publication of the work signifies that it is deemed a competent treatment worthy of public consideration but does not imply endorsement of conclusions or recommendations.

The Institution maintains its position of neutrality on issues of public policy in order to safeguard the intellectual freedom of the staff. Hence interpretations or conclusions in Brookings publications should be understood to be solely those of the authors and should not be attributed to the Institution, to its trustees, officers, or other staff members, or to the organizations that support its research.

EDITOR'S ACKNOWLEDGMENTS

This book presents papers prepared for Employer Participation in School-to-Work Transition Programs, a conference held at the Brookings Institution in May 1994. The conference was organized under the auspices of the Brown Center on Education Policy. In addition to Brown Center funding, the conference also received a generous grant from The German Marshall Fund of the United States.

Henry Aaron, director of the Economic Studies program at Brookings, was responsible for the project and provided necessary help and support. Lois Rice provided help in planning the conference and choosing the speakers and discussants. Anita Whitlock handled administrative responsibilities.

Lisa Rotham and Michelle Cannon of the staff at the Institute on Education and the Economy at Teachers College, Columbia University, provided support and assistance throughout the conference planning and manuscript production stages of the project. Nancy Kunz helped in the final stages. I also want to thank Donna Merritt, my coauthor on the paper that sparked my initial interest in employer participation in school-to-work transition.

Jeffrey King of the German Marshall Fund provided helpful suggestions about both the content and the participants of the conference. I also relied on the advice of Marianne Dourand-Durhael, Jack Jennings, Laurel McFarland, Trish McNeil, Paul Osterman, Cathy Stasz, David Stern, Michael Timpane, Margaret Vickers, Winifred Warnet, Joan Wills, and John Wirt. Phyllis Eisen of the American Manufacturers Association and Peter Joyce of the National Alliance of Business were also helpful in planning the content of the conference and finding participants from the private sector.

It was a pleasure working with the authors, who wrote interesting papers, got them in on time, and were prompt about returning the edited manuscripts. I particularly want to thank Robert Poczik, who agreed to write a paper after the conference when I decided that the important matter of school reform had not been addressed. I also want to thank the discussants, whose contributions, as much as the authors', made the conference a success. These included George Chambliss, Xavier Del Buono, Harry Featherstone, Jack Jennings, John McKernan, Robert Poczik, Stuart Rosenfeld, Anthony Sarmiento, Berndt Söhngen, Cheryl Fields Tyler, Joan Wills, Peter Van den Dool, and Bob Yurasits.

Many people at Brookings worked with the manuscript and contributed to the production of the book. Jim Schneider edited the manuscript; Lisa Guillory, Paige Oeffinger, Colette Solpietro, and Anita Whitlock collated authorial and editorial corrections; and Peter Lindeman typeset it.

Contents

Chapter 1

THOMAS BAILEY

Introduction

In the past decade diagnoses of deficiencies in the U.S. education system have led to a reform strategy generally referred to as school-to-work transition. Although the strategy includes many components, work-based education is a crucial element. Work-based education involves exposing students to real work in real workplaces, but it entails much more than simply providing them with work experience. After all, many teenagers hold jobs while in school, and many reformers believe that these jobs have little educational value. School-to-work strategies call for a planned and structured work experience that has productive educational value and is carefully coordinated with the learning taking place in the classroom.

This book, based on a 1994 conference, addresses the feasibility of work-based education as a large-scale reform of U.S. education, whether the strategy can work for large numbers of students, what political and financial costs are associated with it, how schools might need to change to be able to implement it successfully, what state and federal policies could help promote it, and if it proves difficult to implement, what alternative strategies might achieve similar results. Because the centerpiece of work-based education is to place students in meaningful jobs, recruiting employers is crucial. Thus, the discussions concentrate on approaches and barriers to securing the active participation of employers.

WHAT IS WRONG WITH THE SCHOOLS?

The 1983 publication of *A Nation at Risk* can conveniently demarcate the beginning of the current period of school reform.[1] Reformers had been at work for decades, but in the early 1980s they became increasingly preoccupied with the effects of inadequate education of U.S. workers on the nation's economy, a development that coincided with increasingly competitive economic challenges from Japan, Germany, and other European countries. Schools were failing to prepare the nation's workforce. The reformers first called for a return to a traditional education system that many thought had helped lay the foundation of the postwar U.S. economic boom. The main result was widespread adoption of stricter academic requirements for high school graduation. But these failed to solve the problems.

Reformers next looked at the education systems of America's competitors. They found that in Germany and Japan in particular, the workplace played a crucial role in the education system. Books such as Stephen Hamilton's *Apprenticeship for Adulthood* and frequent study tours for educators, business people, and academics spread information about workplace-based systems.[2] The consensus, as Paul Osterman notes in his chapter of this book, was that U.S. schools were not teaching the skills needed for work and that the transition from school to a stable career-oriented job was a haphazard and disorganized process. After graduating from high school, young people seemed to spend several years moving among low-paying jobs that neither required nor taught many skills. Too much time elapsed before young high school graduates got a chance to use whatever advanced skills they might have learned in school.

Part of the problem seems to be that the secondary school system is too oriented toward preparing students for college; the majority who will never receive a baccalaureate degree are neglected.[3] At least in college-oriented schools, guidance counselors know what college admissions committees want, they know the procedures and deadlines for applications, and they understand the strengths and weaknesses of different postsecondary schools. College admissions committees have a good understanding of the meaning of a record from a particular high school, and they have SATs and other means of evaluating candidates. Although this system works much better in some schools than in others, there is no system remotely comparable to connect high school graduates to local employers. Employers rarely consider the high school records of applicants and, with some exceptions, school staff have little knowledge of potential employers and little contact with them. High school graduates not headed to college are left to drift on their own, exposed primarily to unskilled low-paid jobs and relying on friends, neighbors, or relatives for information about career opportunities. And high school students' awareness that they will end up initially in the same types of jobs (often the same job) that they have had before graduation stifles incentives to work hard in school.

Thus young people know little about work, have no clear idea about what they must do to enter a particular career or occupation, and do not know what might be expected of them at work. They have only the vaguest notions about what skills they need to learn and have no particular incentive to learn those skills—they do not understand how the skills and knowledge they learn in school can benefit them. Meanwhile, schools fail to teach the appropriate attitudes and workplace behavior, and do little to help students achieve the maturity and responsibility they must assume as adult workers. Isolated with their peers both in school and in their "youth" jobs, young people have little contact with adults other than teachers, and the typical student-teacher relationship bears little similarity to effective relationships on the job.

These criticisms of schools have recently been reinforced by increasingly influential research concluding that traditional schooling (academic as well as vocational) prevents the full development of each student's cognitive abilities. Teaching that emphasizes abstract concepts and the transmission of information from student to teacher engages only a few students. Proponents of so-called contextual learning argue that individuals learn skills more effectively if what they learn has a close relationship with their everyday activities. Others suggest that the learning environment needs to reproduce "the technological, social, time, and motivational characteristics of the real work situations in which what is being learned will be used."[4]

Rapidly changing skill requirements also demand educational innovation. Reformers argue that workers at all levels need to be problem solvers. They need to have a deeper understanding of their jobs, be able to function confidently in uncertain and ambiguous situations in which there may be no specific right answer, and be able to work closely with other workers. Traditional schooling, they declare, fails to develop these abilities or characteristics. Students learn skills they need to perform well in schools, but those skills may not serve them well outside school—the learning is not transferred to the community or workplace.[5]

Thus schools are not doing their job because they
—provide no incentive for students to work hard;
—do little to help students find good jobs;

—do not teach the attitudes and maturity needed on the job;

—isolate young people from adults who could act as models and mentors;

—do a poor job of teaching the so-called advanced generic skills or workplace basics such as problem solving and teamwork, and the job-specific skills that are taught atrophy as young people spend a few years churning through unskilled youth jobs; and

—provide a form of schooling that is ineffective in its pedagogic strategy.[6]

To what extent can placement in an appropriately structured work experience overcome the problems I have outlined? Advocates of work-based education suggest four related advantages. It has crucial cognitive benefits, creates necessary institutional linkages between schools and workplaces, provides a unique motivation for students to learn, and can promote the maturity and behavior needed to be an effective worker.

—*Cognitive benefits.* Work-based education is a crucial part of an increasingly popular teaching strategy that emphasizes problem solving, teamwork, learning in context, and more active participation of students in their own learning. Much of this approach can be used in the classroom, but advocates suggest that it works best if students get a chance to learn and use skills in a well-designed work experience. By incorporating education into real-world situations in which what is being learned will be used, work-based education bridges the intellectual or cognitive gap between school and work (or social activity in general). This is a much broader justification for the approach than the argument traditionally advanced by advocates of vocational education that academic schooling does not teach useful or marketable skills. Advocates of work-based education contend that traditional schooling (academic as well as vocational) prevents the full development of each student's cognitive abilities. Thus appropriately organized and structured work-based education is not simply a good way to teach high-quality vocational skills for those not bound for college, but it is a valuable educational strategy for the intellectual development of all students.

—*Institutional linkages.* Work-based education forces schools to forge linkages with workplaces. Such relationships are much less likely to occur in purely school-based reforms. Work-based education also gives students contacts among employers. Thus by moving part of the formal education into the workplace (presumably not primarily in so-called youth-jobs), work-based education breaches the barrier between youth jobs experience and higher-quality employment. Perhaps even more significantly, work-based education creates a formal relationship between employers and schools, promoting a more interactive flow of information.

—*Student motivation.* Work-based education motivates students by showing them how skills are used in real-world settings and how their success and advancement can depend on learning particular skills. Although some students are excited by the learning that dominates much of the traditional curriculum, others are not convinced that they have any use for it. Experience on an appropriate job gives a student an opportunity to use skills gained in class. Not only do students learn that skills are useful on some generic "job," but that they are also crucial steps in a ladder leading to particular jobs and occupations.

—*Maturity and appropriate workplace behavior.* One common criticism of the U.S. labor market is that employers are reluctant to hire adolescents for jobs that carry any significant responsibility. Employers believe young people simply do not know how to behave on the job and that they cannot be counted on. But school-to-work advocates argue that, to the extent employers are correct, the behavior is not surprising because young people, isolated with their peers in school and in youth jobs, have little contact with adults other than their teachers. How can they develop appropriate behavior if they have no models? Experience in the right type of job gives them an intensive experience in a mostly adult environment. The beneficial effects of this may be especially strong if the student works closely with a mentor who not only demonstrates through his or her own behavior how the student should act, but also helps teach the student directly.

Thus, work placement is a crucial component of a reform strategy that confronts some of the major deficiencies of contemporary American education. The chapter by David Stern returns to this issue and discusses alternatives to full work-based education programs for achieving some of these ends. But the urgency of the search for alternatives depends very much on the difficulties and costs associated with its implementation, issues that I take up in the next chapter and that are also addressed in the chapters by Robert Poczik and Margaret Vickers.

The School-to-Work Model

Reformers have advocated a variety of models to address the perceived deficiencies of traditional schooling, and in the late 1980s and
early 1990s, states and many individual schools and school districts
have been experimenting with different approachers. Some of the
lessons from this experience were incorporated into the School-to-
Work Opportunities Act of 1994, and even if the act is not renewed,
reauthorized, or funded in future years, the program model it specifies
can be taken as a general example of the type of reform being developed to address these problems.

According to the act, a comprehensive reform plan must include
three broad components—school-based learning, work-based learning, and connecting activities.

The school-based component, as outlined in the act, emphasizes
student career awareness and career exploration and counseling, fol-
lowed by selection of a career major. It includes a program of study
designed to meet the same academic content standards the state has
established for all students. Program instruction (including applied
methodologies and team teaching strategies) and curriculum integrate
academic and vocational learning. The program also includes regularly scheduled evaluations and procedures to facilitate the entry of students into additional training or postsecondary education programs.

The work-based component includes a planned program of job
training and work experience that is coordinated with learning in the
school-based component, and workplace mentoring. Students receive
instruction in general workplace competencies, including instruction
in and activities related to developing positive work attitudes and
employability and participative skills. The act also lists paid work
experience, job shadowing, school-sponsored enterprise, and on-the-
job training as permissible activities.

The third component of a comprehensive reform plan, according to
the act, is connecting activities. These include matching students with
appropriate work-based learning opportunities and providing a
school-site mentor to act as liaison between the employer and the student's school, teacher, school administrator, and parent. A further
activity is to provide technical assistance to employers and other par-
ties in designing school-based learning components and in training
teachers and workplace mentors and counselors. Assistance to schools
and employers to integrate school-based and work-based learning and

integrate academic and occupational learning must also be supplied. The active participation of employers must be encouraged, and graduates must be assisted in finding a job, continuing their education, or entering into additional training. Youth development activities need to be linked with employer and industry strategies for upgrading the skills of their workers.

Many of these characteristics have been developed in several models, some of which have been common in the United States for many years. The models include cooperative education, career academies, occupational-academic clusters, technical preparation programs, and youth apprenticeship.[7]

Cooperative Education

Cooperative education was developed in the early 1900s. It is defined by the 1990 amendments to the Carl D. Perkins Vocational Education Act of 1984 as "a method of instruction of vocational education for individuals, who, through written cooperative arrangement between the school and employers, receive instruction, including required academic courses and related vocational instruction, by alternation of study in school with a job in any occupational field. Such alternation should be planned and supervised by the school and employers so that each contributes to the student's education and to his or her employability."The quality of these jobs varies, but most include a training plan relevant to the work the student is doing in school. Until very recently, cooperative education has been closely associated with vocational education. The work experience is the core of cooperative education, and the related school-based component is often a traditional vocational education curriculum. There are about 500,000 secondary school students in cooperative education at any given time.[8]

High School Academies

The academy model was established in Philadelphia about 1970 but has spread, most notably to California. There are now more than a hundred academies in the country. Each academy is organized as a school within a school, maintaining a small-school atmosphere within a much larger institution.[9] Each also has a particular occupational or industrial focus, such as electronics, health, or business. The curriculum derives from the focus; instructional techniques include practical and team-based projects. Local employers are involved with the academies, donating equipment and time as advisors and mentors. They also often provide job placements and internships for academy students and graduates. The academy model is built on the principle that the focus on industry gives coherence to the curriculum. Work placements have a clear role in this model, but in practice that role is often not well developed.

Tech-Prep Programs

The central concept of tech-prep (technical preparation) programs is the articulation of secondary school and community college programs in specific occupational areas. Although the concept dates from the late 1960s, the 1990 amendments to the Carl Perkins Act allocated funds to encourage the coordination of curricula during the last two years of high school and two years of community college "with a common core of required proficiency in mathematics, science, communications, and technologies designed to lead to an associate degree or certificate in a specific career field" (section 344). Coordination and consultation with local employers and labor unions are also key components of the model. The concept lends itself to the inclusion of a work component, although many tech-prep programs still have not developed this component.

Occupational-Academic Clusters

Cluster programs are typically large-scale efforts to offer all of the students in a high school a choice among several career pathways, each one based on a sequence of related courses tied to a cluster of occupations (such as environment-related industries, service industries, or manufacturing and engineering occupations). Students are usually exposed to a wide variety of careers before choosing an occupational cluster, and they may switch clusters in the course of the program.

Each cluster offers occupations-related courses; students receive training in broad, work-related skills after taking introductory career exploration courses. Academic and occupational instruction are integrated and applied learning techniques are sometimes used. Work-based experiences enable students to explore potential careers.[10]

The School-to-Work Opportunities Act incorporates the clustering idea, suggesting that students choose one of a small number of clusters at the end of their sophomore year. Oregon is working toward a policy in which all students would be enrolled in such clusters in their junior year, although some clusters are academic rather than occupational. Clustering lends itself to the inclusion of work placement, although that can be a secondary aspect. The breadth of the clusters may make it easier to find placements because a wide range of occupations and jobs may be appropriate for a given cluster.

Youth Apprenticeship

The most ambitious work-based education program among the current school-to-work models is youth apprenticeship, modeled after the German apprenticeship system. Students spend a substantial amount of time in paid work in which they are guided by adult supervisors who work closely with them on job-related and general employment-related skills. In principle, the classroom work, designed to integrate academic and vocational learning, is closely related to the work experience. Youth apprenticeship models also coordinate secondary with postsecondary education. The youth apprenticeship is very demanding on employers. As a result, there are still only a handful of full youth apprenticeship programs nationally, enrolling perhaps 1,000 students.

This is not an exhaustive list of school-to-work models. Various versions of school-based enterprise, restructured traditional vocational education, and expanded career counseling can be grouped under the school-to-work rubric, but in none of these models is job placement a primary concern. The models I have discussed structure learning through an occupational or vocational focus. The approach is designed to use the occupations or industries to provide a context, meaning, and concreteness to the skills. Thus all the models attempt to integrate occupational and vocational learning. Connections to the workplace are created both through employer involvement and school-based counselors who develop work placements and keep in touch with the employers.

All the models also make some attempt to provide work-based education through internships or cooperative placements, although the intensity of the experience varies and is of secondary importance except in cooperative education and youth apprenticeship programs.

Job placements in traditional cooperative education programs often have little to do with in-school learning, and although training plans are common, they rarely lead to a mastery of a coherent sequence of skills. Youth apprenticeships have much more ambitious work-based education components, but there are still only a handful of them in the country. Thus despite strong and reasonable arguments in favor of expanded work-based education, the component remains far more a concept than a reality.

CONCLUSION

Why has a strategy that seems so attractive to many educators, policy-makers, students, and parents been so slow to spread? In some places structural problems within the schools stand in the way. Incorporating work-based components into mainstream education requires changes in school scheduling patterns and reforms in the ways teachers work together. The components challenge traditional divisions between vocational and academic teachers and programs. They also require innovations in teacher preparation and professional development, profound improvements in the quality and nature of counseling, and significant changes in approaches to student assessment and high school graduation requirements. The admission policies of selective colleges are also a barrier to implementation. Colleges generally do not recognize work experience, forcing high schools that focus on college admissions to maintain a more traditional approach to the secondary school curriculum, or to include work-based education only as an add-on program. Thus there is little movement away from traditional education in private schools and elite public high schools. This creates the possibility that the traditional vocational track might simply be replaced with a second-class school-to-work track for students who are not able to make it in the college preparation programs.

Even if solutions to these problems could be found, work-based education will come to nothing if enough work placements are not forthcoming. Developing educationally productive work experience is one of the most challenging problems facing school-to-work program developers. Thus this book focuses on this crucial issue.

One of the main conclusions of the following chapters is that work-based education should not be thought of as one strategy but rather as a continuum of possibilities. There may be a consensus among educators that some form of structured learning on the job that is coordinated with classroom work could be important in the education of many young people, but the consensus provides little practical guidance. Although many may agree that some coherent practical experience can serve an important purpose, there is less agreement about when that experience should take place, who should have it, how long it should last, and how much it is worth.

An impediment to more definitive answers to these questions is that empirical research has so far failed to provide measures of the benefits of work-based education in relation to various types of entirely school-based programs. Case studies contain convincing accounts of benefits, but again quantitative measurements are lacking. Although some research does suggest that academy programs reduce dropout rates and raise test scores, the analysis does not identify the separate effects of the work placements.[11] Analysis of wage gains attributable to cooperative education suggests that higher wages accrue only to those students who stay on in the workplace in which they were placed as students. But most cooperative programs are among the less intensive versions of work-based education, and little is known about how quickly wage gains might rise (if indeed they would) as a work-based education program becomes more intense. Thus research has not been able to provide a definite measure of the benefits of work-based education, although logical arguments, experience abroad, and optimistic reports from pilot projects are strong enough to encourage further experimentation and study.

In addition to surer understanding of the benefits of work-based education, policymakers need more information on the cost of such a program. How difficult would it be to develop an adequate number of high-quality work placements, and what financial and political resources would be needed to implement and sustain work-based education? What other reforms, including school-based education reforms, will have to be forgone to recruit employers?

This book tries to provide a stronger foundation for policy development by addressing some straightforward questions. What barriers stand in the way of employer provision of work placements? Given those problems and the potential benefits, what should the nature of employer participation and work placements be? Are there alternative approaches to achieve the same ends that are less demanding of employer participation? What policies are possible to promote these desired objectives?

In chapter 2, I explore the barriers to employer participation and the incentives they have to provide work placements. In chapter 3, Margaret Vickers explores lessons for participation of employers in the United States by examining employer participation systems in Sweden and Germany. In chapter 4, David Stern considers how employers might be involved other than by providing job placements. In chapter 5, Robert Poczik points out that if employers and the workplace are going to become much more involved with education, schools will have to change to be able to work more effectively with employers and with students in the workplace. In chapter 6, Paul Osterman suggests possible state and federal policies to promote employer involvement. And in chapter 7, I summarize the arguments and the discussion that took place at the conference.

NOTES

1. Commission on Excellence in Education, *A Nation at Risk* (Government Printing Office, 1983).

2. Stephen F. Hamilton, *Apprenticeship for Adulthood: Preparing Youth for the Future* (Free Press, 1990).

3. Perhaps the best-known statement of this position is in the William T. Grant Foundation report, *The Forgotten Half: Pathways to Success for America's Youth and Young Families* (Washington, 1988). Since then, many other studies have pointed out the absence of any system to structure the transition from school to work for those not bound for college. See, for example, General Accounting Office, *Management Practices: US Companies Improve Performance through Quality Efforts*, MSIAD091–190 (1991); and Commission on the Skills of the American Workforce, *America's Choice: High Skills or Low Wages* (Rochester, N.Y.: National Center on Education and the Economy, 1990).

4. See Sue Berryman and Thomas Bailey, *The Double Helix of Education and the Economy* (New York: Institute on Education and the Economy, Teachers College, Columbia University, 1992), for a review.

5. Lauren B. Resnick, "Learning in School and Out," *Educational Researcher*, vol. 16 (December 1987) pp. 13–20; and Senta Raizen, "Reforming Education for Work: A Cognitive Science Perspective," National Center for Research in Vocational Education, University of California, 1989.

6. There is some dissent from this diagnosis. Many labor market economists argue that the so-called churning of young workers is actually productive job

search activity in which they try different jobs, learn what is expected of them, and decide what types of work they might enjoy. Although school-to-work advocates decry the apparent chaos in the youth labor market, others suggest that the lack of structure has promoted flexibility. The much more structured German system is considered rigid and slow to react to increasingly rapid change; see James J. Heckman, Rebecca L. Roselius, and Jeffrey A. Smith, "U.S. Education and Training Policy: A Reevaluation of Underlying Assumptions behind the 'New Consensus,'" Irving B. Harris Graduate School of Policy Studies, University of Chicago, June 1994. Some critics also point out that while apprenticeships keep down unemployment among German youth, joblessness increases at the end of the apprenticeship period. By their late twenties, however, a much larger share of Germans than Americans are in long-term jobs; see Paul Osterman, "Is There a Problem with the Youth Labor Market and If So How Should We Fix It?" Sloan School, MIT, July 1991.

7. The following descriptions are drawn from Thomas Bailey and Donna Merritt, *School-to-Work Transition and Youth Apprenticeship in the United States: Lessons from the U.S. Experience* (New York: Manpower Demonstration Research Corporation, 1993); Edward Pauley, Hillary Kopp, and Joshua Haimson, *Home-Grown Lessons: Innovative Programs Linking Work and High School* (New York: Manpower Demonstration Research Corporation, 1994), pp. xvi, xvii; and David Stern and others, *School to Work: Research on Programs in the United States* (Bristol, Pa.: Palmer Press, 1995).

8. Thomas Bailey, "Can Youth Apprenticeship Thrive in the United States?" *Educational Researcher*, vol . 22 (April 1991), pp. 4–10.

9. Stern and others, *School to Work*.

10. Pauley, Kopp, and Haimson, *Home-Grown Lessons*, p. 7.

11. Stern and others, *School to Work*.

Chapter 2

THOMAS BAILEY

Incentives for Employer Participation in School-to-Work Programs

Work-based education is assuming an increasingly prominent role in education reform. Proponents hope that the School-to-Work Opportunities Act of 1994 will be the first legislative step toward the use of the workplace as a central component of basic education for older adolescents. Even without the support of federal legislation, many states have developed their own initiatives incorporating work-based education. Thus there is a growing conviction among policymakers and educators that some form of structured on-the-job learning coordinated with classroom work can be important in the education of many young people.

But that consensus provides little policy guidance. Work-based education is not a well-defined program but rather a continuum of possibilities. The more ambitious proposals call for intensive learning on the job, linked to a related in-school curriculum and leading to widely recognized and portable skills credentials. More limited plans suggest some exposure to the world of work or even community service. But analysts and educators disagree about what kind of program is best and about such basic matters as when work experience should take place, who should have it, how long it should last, how much it will cost, how much it is worth, and what resources and alternative approaches should be relinquished to implement and sustain it.

Policymakers lack the information they need to choose among the many possible levels of programs. Empirical research has failed to provide measures of the benefits of work-based education in relation to various types of school-based programs. And although case studies contain some convincing accounts of the benefits of work-based education, they too lack quantitative measurements.[1] Nor has research addressed the political and financial resources needed to mount a work-based education program. This chapter focuses on one of the most important determinants of those resources: the willingness of employers to participate in work-based education, particularly by providing work placements. The more ambitious proposals would require developing hundreds of thousands or even millions of work placements. Widespread resistance among employers would obviously increase the financial and political costs needed to develop these placements or indeed to mount any type of work-based education program.

Employer participation involves much more than simply providing jobs for large numbers of young people. Many of course already have jobs. In many work-based models employers would be expected to provide a coherent educational experience coordinated with learning in the classroom, in effect moving part of the public education system into workplaces. This chapter examines the incentives employers have to participate in such work-based education programs and reviews empirical evidence. It also briefly considers the policy implications.

INCENTIVES FOR EMPLOYER PARTICIPATION

If an expanded system of work-based education for secondary and postsecondary school students is to go beyond the type of part-time work millions of teenagers already experience, it needs to do more than simply place young people in any job that can be found. Employers must have some commitment to the broader goals of the public education system.

Why would they be willing to participate? In this chapter I discuss three types of motivation. The first is philanthropic, based on a conviction among employers that they should contribute to the improvement of their communities. The second and third types of motivation are based on employers' self-interest. Participation may be in the direct interest of the individual employer: individual motivation. Or employers may not expect to gain in the short run from their individual participation, but they believe that their industry or occupational group could benefit if many employers participate: collective motivation.

Philanthropic Motivation

Many businesses are willing to work with students and schools out of a sense of corporate responsibility or a commitment to helping their communities. A study of fifteen school-to-work pilot projects found that an interest in helping out their community was one of the two most often cited reasons employers were willing to participate.[2] And another study has found that in a sample of 227 employers participating in cooperative education, most either agree or strongly agree with the statement that they participated in part to perform a community service.[3] This sentiment was overwhelming among companies with more than one hundred workers.

There is no well-defined distinction between philanthropic and self-interest motivations. An employer may believe that improved education would benefit the country as a whole and that in turn would benefit the employer. But it is a long way between the employer's individual actions and the eventual benefit.

The potential limits to employer participation based only on philanthropic motivation are difficult to determine. Philanthropy has undoubtedly been crucial to their involvement in the early stages of school-to-work programs. Most proponents would agree that purely philanthropic motivation would not be adequate to sustain a large and intense work-based education system.

Individual Motivation

Philanthropic motivation has been the foundation of the early growth of the school-to-work programs, but they are more likely to thrive if employers participate because they consider participation to be in their direct individual interest. After all, employers hire and train workers, and perhaps those workers might be young people in school-to-work programs. Individual employers could derive various benefits from participation. First, there is a public relations benefit. Second, school-to-work programs could be a source of low-cost labor. Finally, students are potentially future employees, and training costs associated with school-to-work programs could thus be considered investments in the future operation of the firm.

Public Relations. By participating in work-based education programs, employers may gain some good will and improved public relations.[4] This is an important reason employers in Germany, especially in small towns, hire apprentices.[5]

But the public relations benefits can probably be achieved with a small number of placements and through programs that do not

demand a great deal from employers. In a study of cooperative education, Irene Lynn and Joan Wills found that even very large firms provide only a few slots.[6] Similarly, Edward Pauley, Hillary Kopp, and
Joshua Haimson found that in twelve of the fifteen sites they examined
in their study of school-to-work pilot projects, employers, most of
whom were large, hired an average of fewer than three trainees.[7]
Many of the participating employers had the organizational capacity
to expand their participation significantly, but these authors suggested
that further expansion would not serve any additional public relations
benefit.

Source of Low-Cost Labor. Employers might also participate in a work-
based education program because they consider trainees or interns a
good source of low-cost labor. The special apprenticeship wage in
Germany, for instance, appears to provide an important incentive for
smaller employers.

But the wage structure is much more regulated in Germany than in
the United States. For many occupations, German employers must pay
workers a regulated skilled wage unless the workers are registered
apprentices, who receive a lower but still negotiated wage. In the
United States unionized construction employers working on federally
funded projects have a similar incentive to hire apprentices: they must
pay skilled wages (usually negotiated through collective bargaining)
to all workers in some occupations with the exception of registered
apprentices. And low-paid interns are an important part of the economics of large teaching hospitals. But outside of these regulated
areas, U.S. employers need no special legal rights to pay low wages as
long as they are at least as high as the legislated minimum wage.

One-quarter of the U.S. employers in the study of cooperative education by Lynn and Wills stated that participation was a way to fill
part-time positions, and a few said they saw the program as "a good
way to get good, lower-paid part-time help."[8]

But, according to Pauley, Kopp, and Haimson, employers participating in recent youth apprenticeship and school-to-work pilot programs, which require more of employers than do cooperative education
programs, complained that there was a high supervisory cost for
trainees and apprentices.[9] Indeed, Alan Hershey and Marsha Silverberg
have argued that employers consider this a greater barrier to participation than the cost of the trainee wages.[10] Because of the disincentives

created by supervisory costs, Pauley, Kopp, and Haimson suggested that schools avoid sending students for placement who might be difficult to supervise, although they warn that too much screening would defeat the objective that the reform serve a broad range of students.

The significance of supervisory costs seems confirmed by evidence from programs that offered subsidies to employers to hire students. During the 1970s, the Youth Entitlement Demonstration program guaranteed jobs for high school students who stayed in school, but the program operators found it difficult to recruit employers. When they surveyed a sample of them in the demonstration areas, they found that only 10 percent were willing to participate if they had to pay 25 percent of the wages of the youth. Potential participation rose to 18 percent if the entire amount of the wage were subsidized, but this still meant that not even one in five of the employers was willing to take on these youth even at a wage of zero.[11] Apparently they believed that the students would not contribute enough to justify the effort needed to supervise them.

Source of Future Workers. There is some evidence that employers do provide slots for work placements with the objective of recruiting future workers. Lynn and Wills found that most of the 270 employers sampled who were participating in cooperative education programs agreed or strongly agreed that the programs were a good source of entry-level workers. Nearly one-half had retained students as employees after the program term had ended. Pauley, Kopp, and Haimson also found that employers participated in the pilot projects to help recruit an adequate labor force.

Recruitment and screening invite at least some employer participation, although these functions could probably be accomplished through a short program without much training. Indeed, the programs that Lynn and Wills studied did not have strong training components. Most did have training plans, but the plans were not effectively implemented.

Certain features of the U.S. labor market, especially in regard to teenagers, reduce the probability that employers will see work-based education students as future employees. High turnover among young workers in particular discourages this view, although more training might induce young people to stay with a company.

In focus groups with employers who were not participating in school-to-work programs, Robert Zemsky found that weak demand for young workers was one of the most important disincentives for participation.[12] These employers had poor opinions of young workers, stating that young recruits wanted to make high wages but were not willing to accept that as new hires with few skills and little experience they were not worth much to the employers. Workers with this attitude were not expected to have enough stability to gain skills and eventually pay back the employer's investment. Businesses that were interested in developing a skilled workforce through training were able to find older, more experienced (and presumably more reliable) workers, often among their own employees. But in any event, current employer training practices for production workers do not provide much basis for optimism about program participation. Even older production workers receive little training. Most company-based training in this country goes to managerial, sales, and professional workers.[13]

A related problem is that although the School-to-Work Opportunities Act states that programs should prepare students for further education as well as future work, many reformers want to avoid the perpetuation of a tracking system in which good students are prepared for college and less successful ones are tracked into school-to-work programs. It is therefore important to design school-to-work systems so that they too can lead to further education. But this design may lead many work-based education students to pursue higher education, thus reducing the incentives for employers to train them.

Despite the absence of strong incentives for employer participation, researchers have found reasons for optimism. Lynn and Wills found that the Federal Aviation Administration had had a positive experience with a "large long-term coop program that [had] been the source of 25 percent of their total regional workforce for several years. Over its twenty years of existence, it [had] been evaluated several times and found to be cost effective as a recruitment vehicle because it decreased turnover." In general in their survey, more than 90 percent of the employers stated that cooperative education students were productive workers and the employers were "well satisfied" with them.[14]

Indeed, comparing the disapproval among nonparticipating employers in his focus groups to the much more favorable opinions of participating employers reported by Lynn and Wills, Zemsky contended that first-hand experience with the programs gave employers a much more constructive perspective.[15] Although the cooperative education programs studied by these researchers were not as intensive as some proposed work-based programs, the results suggest that as experience with these programs grows, more employers will at least begin to have neutral views about participation.

Nevertheless, employers continue to have a variety of other options for recruiting and screening applicants and upgrading their workforce. They can put more effort into recruiting more skilled workers or they can provide training for workers who have already demonstrated some loyalty or commitment to the company. There certainly may be circumstances in which work-based education programs coincide with the interests of employers, but given the traditional operation of the youth labor market in this country, it seems likely that the direct and individual interests of employers will provide a weak basis for a broad work-based education system.

COLLECTIVE MOTIVATION

One of the most common arguments for improving education in the United States is that employers lack a skilled labor force. Newspapers frequently carry accounts of companies that have had to screen hundreds of applicants to fill a handful of job openings. In some areas manufacturers have difficulty attracting young people willing to devote time to learning skills because of the general impression that the industries are declining and future opportunities are limited. Employers in rural areas may also have trouble finding skilled workers. Thus it is in the interest of industries that are facing these circumstances to promote the development of a skilled labor force. But individual employers will be reluctant to invest in training because they could lose the workers they train. They want a strengthened pool, not a few workers trained in job-specific skills. This situation invites collective action.

Recent research has demonstrated that employers are willing to contribute to strengthening their industry's labor pool. Many managers have stated that they participate in school-to-work pilot projects for the benefit of the entire industry or profession.[16] Inherent in this perspective is the realization that a company may not benefit directly in the long term from its own trainees but that broad implementation of work-based programs would strengthen the labor supply for all the industry's employers.

An industry or occupational focus could also be important for work-based programs because it would harmonize with the objective articulated in the Goals 2000: Educate America Act to establish industry skill standards that would lead to portable skills certification. Indeed, standards and certification could play a crucial role in providing support for work-based education. If employers had confidence that a reliably certified pool of skilled workers was available, they might be less fearful about losing the individual workers they had trained.

Although collective incentives have the potential to support a broad work-based system, they can only do so if there is an appropriate institutional framework through which collective interests can be articulated and regulated. Without this framework, individual firms will still have little incentive to participate. For example, employers could continue to benefit from a pool of certified skilled workers even if they did not participate in the system that trained and certified the workers. Full participation is probably not necessary, but such a system requires a critical mass.

This situation opens up crucial opportunities for employer organizations and for unions. The importance of these social partners in European school-to-work systems is well known.[17] And U.S. employer organizations have become increasingly supportive of school-to-work strategies and associated efforts to improve industry skill standards.[18] To the extent that work-based education programs strengthen an industry as a whole, it is clearly in the interest of employer organizations to promote them.

Unions, too, have an interest in promoting the health of the industry, although they are also concerned with the employment effects of work-based education systems. Especially in industries with declining or stagnant employment, providing work placements for young people may seem to threaten adult jobs.[19] Although unions may oppose work-based education for this reason, the problem also gives them a potentially important opportunity to work with employers to try to prevent adult loss of jobs and encourage support for work-based education among older workers.

The construction apprenticeship system offers a good example of the importance of a collective regulatory framework. This system appears to produce broadly skilled workers through training that mostly takes place on the job. It benefits both the industry and the construction occupations by providing a pool of skilled and experienced labor and illustrates the importance of the legal and institutional framework through which the collective interests can be furthered.

The construction labor market is highly regulated because of the continuing influence of unions and the prevalence of federally funded projects, in which employers must pay the skilled wage rate to all workers, regardless of their actual skill level, except for registered apprentices, who can be paid lower wages. Most apprenticeship programs in construction are administered jointly by unions and employer associations according to requirements in collective bargaining agreements. The cost and responsibility for apprenticeship training, curriculum planning, and testing is divided among them. Thus workers and their representatives are directly involved in defining the necessary skills and overseeing apprentice certification.

But the construction programs, despite their success, have never been suggested as a model for school-to-work systems, probably because a system based on collective bargaining and government regulation of wages and employment conditions does not seem politically feasible. Furthermore, construction has devised coherent industry and occupational definitions and boundaries. Other industries may not lend themselves to such clear technical definitions.

The construction industry also illustrates another potential problem with employer incentives, even collective incentives, for participation. The industry's effective work-based education system does serve the collective interests of employers, but it does not primarily serve adolescents. Construction apprentices are usually in their late twenties, and many are high school graduates. And to the extent that work-based education programs can be (some proponents say should be) a route to further education, construction and other industries would be less interested in mounting a large-scale system for training young workers. For an employer it may make more sense to train older workers who are considered more stable and more likely to stay in the industry.[20]

Thus in some industries and labor markets, employers do have a collective interest in organizing a training system, but even under these circumstances, this interest may not lead to a work-based education system for teenagers. A collective system is unlikely to develop without an appropriate legal and institutional framework. And measures need to be taken so that the system serves young people and addresses the broader objectives of the public education system.

CONCLUSION

It is perhaps ironic that while anxiety about productivity and competitiveness have pushed educators and policymakers in the direction of devising a work-based education system, the same economic factors do not provide strong incentives for employers to participate. A widespread work-based program with significant education for large numbers of adolescents occurring in real workplaces does not seem likely if it must count primarily on the unaided self-interest of individual employers. If work-based strategies are to be important in education, public policy must bring the interests of employers into line with those broader objectives. Another chapter in this book addresses the matter more thoroughly, but I will make two observations here.

First, an industry- or occupation-oriented approach to reasonably intensive work-based education seems much more likely to succeed if it is founded on employers' collective rather than their individual interests. The school-business partnerships so necessary for such a system depend first then on business-business partnerships. (Business-labor partnerships could also be important, although their effect is limited in a country where only one-tenth of the workforce is organized.) An implementation policy that encourages employers to act together may then be more effective than general subsidies, tax credits, or other policies that focus on individual incentives.

From the perspective developed here, pilot projects funded in the mid-1990s by the Departments of Labor and Education to develop industry-based skill standards take on particular significance as test cases. In the development and implementation of these standards, groups of employers and educators will have to confront many of the same obstacles that they will face as they work toward a work-based education system.

A second consideration for enrolling employer interest is the trade-off between the intensity of a work-based education program and the efforts and extra incentives needed to recruit employers. Usually, the more intense the program, the greater the effort. One of the more optimistic conclusions from recent empirical studies of employer participation comes from Lynn and Wills's survey of employers participating in cooperative programs. Many employers said they would be willing to expand their placements if they were asked. The study also found that program counselors were able to find enough placements for interested students. But the programs were much less ambitious than many current proposals. The less the strategy expects from employers, the more likely they are to be willing to participate—whether that participation is based on individual or collective motivations.

What then is the optimal mix of intensity and participation? How much intensity needs to be sacrificed to attract how many employers? What is the additional benefit to students of a given increment of program intensity? Which students will benefit? How can public policy affect the nature of the trade-off and at what political or financial cost, or both? Are there in-school teaching strategies that can either achieve some of the benefits of work-based education or at least enhance the educational value of less intensive work-based strategies or of placements in less skilled jobs? Will a determined effort to recruit reluctant employers divert attention from other needed educational reforms, especially those within the schools themselves? Unfortunately, a great deal more has to be known before we can answer these questions. And the answers need to be found as policymakers apply the framework established by the School-to-Work Opportunities Act to specific programs at the state level.

In the final assessment, the incentives for employer participation in school-to-work programs are weak. There are possibilities for building a stronger foundation for participation, but the task of developing the needed policy has only just begun.

NOTES

1. See chapter 1 for a fuller discussion of empirical evidence on the effects of work-based education.

2. Edward Pauley, Hillary Kopp, and Joshua Haimson, *Home-Grown Lessons: Innovative Programs Linking Work and High School* (San Francisco: Jossey-Bass, 1995).

3. Irene Lynn and Joan Wills, *School Lessons, Work Lessons: Recruiting and Sustaining Employer Involvement in School-to-Work Programs* (Washington: Institute on Educational Leadership, 1994).

4. This differs from philanthropic motivation because employers do expect to derive some individual benefit from goodwill on the part of local community members.

5. Wolfgang Franz and David Soskice, "The German Apprenticeship System," Discussion Paper (Berlin: Social Science Research Center, 1994).

6. Lynn and Wills, *School Lessons, Work Lessons.*

7. Pauley, Kopp, and Haimson, *Home-Grown Lessons.*

8. Lynn and Wills, *School Lessons, Work Lessons*, p. 29.

9. Pauley, Kopp, and Haimson, *Home-Grown Lessons.*

10. Alan Hershey and Marsha Silverberg, "Employer Involvement in School-to-Work Transition Programs: What Can We Really Expect?" paper prepared for a conference of the Association for Public Policy and Management, Washington, 1993.

11. Joseph Ball and others, "Participation of Private Businesses as Work Sponsors in the Youth Entitlement Demonstration" (New York: Manpower Demonstration Research Corporation, 1981).

12. Robert Zemsky, "What Employers Want: Employer Perspectives on Youth, the Youth Labor Market, and Prospects for a National System of Youth Apprenticeships," Working Paper 22, National Center on Educational Quality of the Workforce, University of Pennsylvania, 1994.

13. Roger Vaughan and Sue Berryman, "Employer-Sponsored Training: Current Status, Future Possibilities," Institute on Education and the Economy, Columbia University, 1989; and Hong Tan, "Private Sector Training in the United States: Who Gets It and Why?" Institute on Education and the Economy, Columbia University, 1989.

14. Lynn and Wills, *School Lessons, Work Lessons*, pp. 29–30.

15. The focus groups conducted by Zemsky and the survey carried out by Lynn and Wills were part of a coordinated research program.

16. Pauley, Kopp, and Haimson, *Home-Grown Lessons.*

17. Robert W. Glover and Alan Weisberg, "School-to-Work Transition in the U.S.: The Case of the Missing Social Partners," Center for Learning and Competitiveness, University of Maryland, 1994.

18. Patricia McNeil, "The Role of Industry Associations in School to Work Transition" (New York: Manpower Demonstration Research Corporation, 1993).

19. Hershey and Silverberg, "Employer Involvement in School-to-Work Transition Programs."

20. Thomas Bailey, "Can Youth Apprenticeship Thrive in the United States?" *Educational Researcher*, vol. 22 (April 1993), pp. 4–10.

Chapter 3

MARGARET VICKERS

Employer Participation in School-to-Work Programs: The Changing Situation in Europe

Many educational reformers are now convinced that America's youth would benefit greatly from a structured system of work-based education that would invigorate the high school curriculum and improve the transition from high school to work or further study. Although the rationale for such a system is based partly on research on the value of contextualized learning and partly on evidence about the difficulties young people experience in finding a good, career-oriented job, arguments for the feasibility of such a system are strongly influenced by the experience of European employers, who are instrumental in developing and sustaining national programs for school-to-work transition.

In Britain, Denmark, France, Germany, Austria, Switzerland, and Sweden (the list is not exhaustive), employers participate collectively and individually in designing and delivering vocational training. Of these, the German apprenticeship system has had the strongest influence on U.S. policy discussions. Texts in English describing the system are readily available, and in the past five years, because of substantial organized support, many education reformers, business people, and politicians have participated in study tours that feature the German system.

The emergence of new arrangements for vocational education in other European countries suggests that the German approach represents only one way among many to encourage employer participation in school-to-work programs. For example, developments in Britain and Sweden have given employers significant responsibilities in the design and delivery of such programs. This chapter discusses these two because each operates differently and employers in each take on distinctly different roles.

Two ideas from Thomas Bailey's chapter on employer incentives for participation are pivotal to this discussion. The first is the distinction between the individual and collective motivations of employers. Although it may not be in the interests of individual employers to help develop a school-to-work system or to provide training places, it may be in the collective interests of their industry to ensure that some critical level of participation is achieved. Thus it might make sense for an employer organization to subsidize the costs incurred by individual employers who do provide training places, particularly if the result of their participation benefits the whole industry.

In Britain, for example, a particular industry may benefit from the work of a handful of representatives who help establish industrywide standards and systems of portable credentials. Alternatively, in Sweden employers (and unions) collaborate with education authorities in shaping relevant components of the high school curriculum. In Germany, the productive sector as a whole benefits from the participation of employer organizations and unions in the development of national training regulations. The regulations promote comparability in the content of the on-the-job training provided by different companies and ensure the portability of apprenticeship qualifications.

The second key idea Bailey introduced concerns the trade-off between the intensity of work-based education and the extent of employer participation. He suggests that if more is asked of each employer, fewer employers will participate. By any measure, the German apprenticeship system is highly intense. Although youth apprenticeship programs inspired by this model might be established on an experimental basis, it may prove impossible to expand such experiments into national or even statewide systems.

The German system demands collective employer participation in designing and implementing national apprenticeship regulations. In addition, all individual employers who provide apprenticeship places must provide a planned program of on-the-job training, complementary off-the-job classes (which are sometimes provided within the company), at least three days a week of full-time employment, and wages on an agreed scale. One-quarter of Germany's employers meet these stipulations. But as Mari Sako argues, the behavior of German employers can only be understood in terms of uniquely German historical and cultural traditions that would be difficult to replicate elsewhere.[1]

The model of upper-secondary education introduced in Sweden in the 1990s provides a less intense and possibly more transferable alternative than the German model. It clusters hundreds of occupational categories into fourteen broad groups, which is particularly relevant to developments in the United States. Clustering is increasingly popular in many states as they develop school-to-work plans. Although this model is attractive, definitive evaluations of its effectiveness are not yet available. Meanwhile, in England and Scotland employer participation has focused on creating a national system of industry-based portable vocational qualifications. It is a broad-based national system, but perhaps it has gone too far in the direction of sacrificing intensity for scale.

GERMANY: EMPLOYERS, THE APPRENTICESHIP SYSTEM, AND THE CHALLENGES OF CHANGE

Building on medieval traditions in which the meisters carefully inducted apprentices into the craft guilds, the German apprenticeship system began as an entirely company-based system. In the early 1900s, it began to be supplemented by attendance at vocational schools, and the dual system was born.[2] Reflecting its origins, employers and meisters remain the senior partners in the system; the part-time vocational schools (Berufsschule) have relatively junior status. Apprentices spend three or four days a week at work and one or two days at school. They are indentured under contract to particular firms; their status is closer to that of a trainee-worker than a student.[3]

The dual system serves more than 60 percent of youth 16 to 19 years old and provides respected entry-level qualifications for some 370 occupations covered by federal apprenticeship regulations.[4] At the end of a program an apprentice must be ready to hold a skilled job: to plan work, do it, and control it.[5] For each of the covered occupations there are frameworks that describe the skills an apprentice should master to gain entry-level qualifications. Although these frameworks leave room for adaptation and negotiation at the local level to ensure that they deliver the skills most relevant to a particular company, the broad kinds of expertise an apprentice needs are clearly spelled out by the frameworks.

The regulations that structure the apprenticeship system mirror the structure of the German labor market. There is an understood professionalism in relation to each of the recognized occupations (berufe), with clear expectations about the kinds of expertise qualified workers should possess, appropriate working conditions, and agreements on wages and remuneration.[6] For skilled workers, their berufe is an important part of their identity, and they continue to build and develop their professional expertise throughout their working life. In most English-speaking countries this sense of "professionalism" is most clearly associated with doctors, lawyers, and other highly qualified white-collar workers.[7]

Regional craft chambers and chambers of industry and commerce are responsible for local implementation of the dual system. They register each apprenticeship contract, certify trainers, inspect training premises, supervise training programs, establish examination boards, organize final exams, and train examiners.[8] The chambers are organized at the local level but provide information that directly influences the work of the state- and federal-level employer organizations.

At the national level the Federal Institute for Vocational Training (BiBB) coordinates the system. The governing board represents four groups—employer organizations, unions, the federal government, and the state (länder) education ministries. With their advice, BiBB establishes regulations (Ausbildungsregulungen) that apply across the whole of Germany. Because these regulations establish common standards, the certificates apprentices are awarded at the end of their training are portable throughout the nation.[9]

The Ausbildungsregulungen coordinate the activities of thousands of training firms across Germany. These regulations constitute a national curriculum for on-the-job training and are treated with utmost seriousness by employer organizations, chambers, and unions. Where local enterprises cannot provide some of the required training, employer organizations and chambers are expected to set up intercompany training centers to deliver the missing components.[10] For example, the introduction of automation and computer numerical control technologies in large, high-technology companies has made it difficult to provide hands-on training on the production line. An increasing trend in these situations is to establish classrooms and simulated work environments within firms or in intercompany training centers.

Although the federal government is responsible for regulating the on-the-job component of apprenticeships, responsibility for the vocational schools lies with the länder. Because curricula are developed cooperatively by the federal and länder governments, schools and firms can articulate their programs semester by semester.[11] Within a given semester, apprentices should find that similar topics and skills are being covered by firms in which they work and in schools they attend. This articulation does not, however, correspond to what some American innovators are attempting to achieve through the integration of school-based and work-based learning. The German system makes no attempt to "integrate" academic and vocational education.[12]

Although the level of voluntary employer compliance with the federal training regulations is astonishing, a complex administrative infrastructure underlies and supports this behavior. Membership in the chambers that inspect training premises, supervise apprenticeship programs, and conduct the final examinations is mandatory for all commercial enterprises.[13] Compliance with apprenticeship regulations is not universal, however; only one-quarter of all companies provide apprenticeship training.[14] These firms generally train more apprentices than they keep and therefore have the advantage of being able to select the best.

Standardized credentials and regulatory infrastructures also provide clear incentives for youth participation in the system. Successful completion of an apprenticeship certificate is a prerequisite for employment as a journeyman (geselle) or a skilled worker (facharbeiter), who receive negotiated wages at standard rates that are among the highest in Europe for equivalent forms of work. An apprenticeship certificate is also a prerequisite for qualification as a meister, a status that may be attained only after several years of work experience and completion of further examinations. Finally, it is also a prerequisite for admission to upper-level technical colleges (fachschulen) and to the special secondary schools that prepare adults for university admission.[15]

Regulation of wages also creates incentives for employers to hire apprentices. A first-year apprentice can expect to receive 25 or 30 percent of the entry-level wage for a qualified worker in a given occupation. Second- and third-year apprentices may receive a little more, but on average an apprentice's wage is typically less than one-third that of a skilled worker. At such low wages a productive apprentice may cover the costs incurred by his or her employer. Recent studies of the financing of the apprenticeship system have contended that employers in small craft firms (who have relatively low training costs) may actually break even.[16]

Most large industrial companies incur significant net costs in training apprentices: in 1994 the estimate for one firm was $3,782 per apprentice.[17] Social scientists who have tried to explain why these companies are willing to make such large investments in training have concluded that apprenticeships reduce subsequent training costs and provide information about the apprentices. But it is the institutional structure of the German labor market that best explains why German companies are motivated to hire apprentices.[18]

Despite the supportive institutional environment and the historical success of the dual system, German educators are no longer expressing unalloyed confidence in its future viability. According to Ute Laur-Ernst, director of BiBB's Department of Educational Technology and Comparative Studies, proponents still emphasize the high quality of the system, but critics contend that its potential for innovation is spent.[19] The critics cite evidence that fewer employers are willing to provide training places and fewer young people are moving through apprenticeships directly into full-time, entry-level employment. The reduction in the numbers of employers providing training is hitting some industries much harder than others. In part, this may be due to a cyclical downturn in certain sectors, but variation in the net costs of sustaining apprenticeships in companies of different sizes and in different sectors also needs to be considered.

In the prestigious motor, engineering, electrical, and steel industries (which together constitute the metalworking group) there has been a statistical reduction in the number of apprenticeship positions offered during the past two years.[20] Recessionary conditions have led to substantial downsizing, employers laid off half a million metalworking employees during 1993, and more closures and layoffs have been announced by some of Germany's largest industrial firms.[21] In this context, recruitment is falling: the number of apprentices being trained by Siemens fell from 3,000 in 1987 to 1,800 in 1993.

Because of this economic downturn, the pattern of close cooperation between IG Metall, Germany's biggest union, and Gesamtmetall, the metalworking employers' federation, has come under increasing strain. Training in large metalworking companies is costly, and skilled technicians are expensive to employ.[22] Labor-management negotiations threaten to loosen some training regulations and blur the distinctions between salaried technicians and skilled workers on hourly wages.[23] The implications for the future of apprenticeship recruitment are serious because the framework agreements between these two organizations represent 12.5 percent of all dual-system training contracts.[24]

Smaller percentages of youth are now choosing to move through apprenticeships into full-time, entry-level employment. The reasons for this are complex and difficult to understand without a detailed knowledge of the structures of secondary and postsecondary education in Germany, but it appears that an increasing proportion of young people are interested in pursuing full-time academic study rather than entering the dual system at age 16.[25] A larger proportion of students now seeks to enter the more academic Gymnasien or the Realschules while few seek entry to the Hauptschule. In the final grade of the Gymnasien, students take the arbitur exams; they may then seek entry into the universities or the higher-level technical institutes. Students may also enter higher-level technical institutes by taking a pathway through the Realschules (middle-level, lower-secondary schools) to the Fachoberschules (technical upper-secondary schools). In 1993 a record 50 percent of Germany's school leavers sought to enter the higher-level technical institutes or the universities.[26]

Still, enrollments in apprenticeships have not fallen as dramatically as these figures might suggest. One-fifth of those who sit for the Arbitur subsequently enter an apprenticeship.[27] At the age of 23 or so, some of these enter the workplace, but many go on to the universities and higher-level technical institutes. Students who follow this relatively new pathway through the education and training system actually complete an Arbitur, an apprenticeship, *and* a higher diploma or a degree before they enter the workforce.

The willingness of so many young people to follow this long and arduous pathway from school to work reflects the breakdown of the traditional promotion system in German companies. In the past a talented German worker could rely on progressing from apprentice to skilled worker to manager. Today, however, executives show a growing tendency to recruit highly qualified people from outside the firm for coveted managerial posts. In this competitive environment, applicants with higher education degrees as well as apprenticeship qualifications usually achieve executive positions much more rapidly than those who climb the ladder the traditional way.[28] Many senior managers in Germany's banks and manufacturing firms can still boast that they began their careers as apprentices, that they attended only the vocational schools, and that they rose from the factory floor to the boardroom. Today, thoughtful observers fear that these senior managers may represent the last of their line.[29]

The German apprenticeship system represents a historically stable partnership between schools and workplaces, but it is one in which employers clearly have the upper hand. While government and unions play key roles, the system is essentially driven by the collective self-regulation of employer organizations. Evidence of emerging strains suggests that the dual system, which has been in place for more than 90 years, may need substantial reform as this century draws to a close.

SWEDEN: EMPLOYER PARTICIPATION IN VOCATIONAL EDUCATION

Unlike the German system, the Swedish apprenticeship system declined in importance between the 1950s and the 1970s, and school-based vocational and technical education and training became the dominant mode. In the new Swedish model, however, employer organizations have a substantial influence over the curriculum in the upper secondary school. In recent reforms the upper-secondary vocational and technical system has been reorganized into fourteen broad pathways, and an on-the-job component has been added, making work-based education a requirement for all students in upper-secondary vocational programs.

Schooling in Sweden is divided into two stages. Compulsory education starts at 7 years of age and finishes at 16 with the award of the general school certificate. Ninety-six percent of each youth cohort goes on to the upper-secondary school. Half follow a vocational program and the other half academic programs; 90 percent graduate.[30] Until 1991, upper-secondary education lasted three years for academic studies and two for those entering the vocational lines, but reforms enacted between 1991 and 1993 extended the duration of the vocational programs to three years as well.[31]

Until 1991 the National Board of Education developed Sweden's national curricula, dictated course content, set standards, and created the student assessment tests. After the reforms of 1991–93 the board was replaced by the National Agency for Education. The agency radically revised upper-secondary schooling. Among other reforms, the agency reduced the number of vocational lines, introduced a work-based learning requirement for all students in vocational pathways in the upper-secondary school, and increased the participation of employers in defining occupational clusters and developing corresponding curricula.

From the 1970s to the 1990s, young people entering vocational programs in the upper-secondary school were required to choose among the 300 occupationally specific lines defined by the National Board of Education. By the 1990s it had become evident that the lines were too narrowly focused. In firms where technological and structural changes demanded that workers possess skills from two or more occupational lines, it was becoming difficult to match entry-level workers with job opportunities.

From 1991 to 1994, representatives of employer organizations and unions collaborated with educators to create 14 new vocational programs, each of which covers a broadly defined occupational field or cluster. The major difficulty in reducing the 300 lines to 14 programs was to bring unions and employer organizations from various occupational groups together and ask them to combine forces. To construct the new curriculum for the energy program, for instance, electricians, power station engineers, and heating and ventilating technicians had to create a program of study that incorporated skills and concepts from all three fields.

Sweden's new upper-secondary curriculum stipulates that students in vocational concentrations must spend at least 15 percent of their time in workplaces.[32] This unpaid work experience is organized in the form of projects designed collaboratively by employer groups and vocational teachers, who discuss the content they consider important and the activities they regard as feasible. In this way they seek to create work-based learning activities consistent with the curriculum frameworks established by the National Agency for Education.

In some regions, municipalitywide coordinators organize the supply of work-based learning places. Coordinators establish the necessary links between schools and companies and help teachers and employers to create integrated learning programs. In Stockholm and other large cities, however, individual schools may make their own arrangements with local firms.[33] Arrangements for work-based learning have been established for each of the fourteen occupational areas covered by the curriculum frameworks. Schools also provide mentor training programs for local employers.

Employers provide placements for students on a voluntary basis, but the opportunity to hire young workers (whose participation is overseen by the schools) may be an incentive to get involved. Although there are no national data, anecdotal evidence suggests that many schools find it difficult to recruit enough employers, so work placements are not always available to the 50 percent of upper-secondary students who have chosen a vocational program. The recessionary conditions that have predominated in Sweden during the early 1990s have made this problem worse.

The reforms of 1991–93 decentralized control over the curriculum, reduced the gap between academic and vocational education, and increased employer participation in the design and delivery of upper-secondary vocational and technical education.[34] Modular courses and flexible study plans have replaced the prescribed vocational and academic curricula of the past, and students take a common core of courses in both the vocational and the academic concentrations.

At the national level, employer organizations and unions have been crucial in the development of fourteen curriculum frameworks. The Ministry of Education assumes the responsibility of setting up working groups to develop curricula, and representatives of the national employers' federation (SAF) are active members of each group. The SAF member may be a full-time federation staff member rather than a current employer. (Membership in the federations is not mandatory, but most employers are members.)

This national activity has helped structure the participation of employers at the local level. For example, nationally developed frameworks provide broad guidelines for the schools, but some modules in the new curricula are created at the municipal level through the cooperative activity of employers and educators.[35]

Why did Sweden's educational policymakers reject the introduction of a German-style apprenticeship system? First, the old Swedish apprenticeship system had never been as large or as inclusive as the German system. In addition, it was not popular. In its original form the system had bonded young people to continue working for their employers after completing their apprenticeships. These conditions were considered an inappropriate restriction on choice and individual opportunity, and educators believed programs based in public schools could better serve the students' interests. Thus after the early 1970s, the apprenticeship system was scaled down; by the late 1980s it was mainly operating in the construction trades and in a handful of crafts.[36]

In the late 1980s, policymakers at the National Board of Education decided that attempting to construct a complex infrastructure like the one that supports the German apprenticeship system would not be wise. According to Anita Ferm, an NBE policymaker at the time, "The discussion was that the Germans have had apprenticeships for a long time, and people inside German enterprises learned their own jobs that way. It would take many years for Swedish enterprises to learn that they might benefit from an apprenticeship system."[37] NBE policymakers also estimated that a German-style apprenticeship system would cost companies four times as much as the system of work-based education that has now been introduced.[38]

The new Swedish framework for work-based learning has much in common with the alternance system introduced by France in the mid-1980s to complement classroom learning in the lycées professionelles (upper-secondary vocational schools). The idea behind alternance is that students have alternating periods of learning, some at school and some at work. Ideally, their experiences in the workplace will help them understand the relevance of their classroom studies. Young people in these programs are students, not apprentices in the German sense, because there are no contracts of employment. Because they are students, they are not paid for their time at the work site, and educators (rather than employers) are the senior partners in curriculum design and program implementation.

Four lessons stand out from the Swedish example. First, occupational clustering appears to have strong support among Swedish educators and employers, suggesting that it is a viable way to organize vocational education at the secondary level. Second, it is difficult to find adequate numbers of job placements for all students in vocational programs, even though the internships are unpaid. Third, Sweden's business federations have taken a lead in setting national standards by participating in developing the new upper-secondary curricula. Finally, employer involvement is provided primarily through representatives from business federations rather than by asking individual firms to volunteer employee time. Federation staff members are familiar with the needs of firms because they have experience as employers or employees themselves. Their service on the curriculum working groups for defined periods is paid for through the federation and is part of their regular job. This model, which not only sets standards but also provides the wherewithal for skill formation, is worth emulating.

GREAT BRITAIN: EMPLOYERS, EMPLOYER ORGANI-
ZATIONS, AND NATIONAL SKILLS STANDARDS

The current arrangements for employer participation in work-based education in Great Britain can be traced to the first version of the youth training scheme (YTS1), launched in 1983. At a time of high youth unemployment, YTS1 was intended to provide basic training and support for young people experiencing difficulty entering the labor market. It provided one year of subsidized work experience to 16-year-old school leavers and unemployed 16- and 17-year-olds. These subsidies encouraged employers to offer training both on and off the job. In theory the quality of YTS1 training was guaranteed by Manpower Services Commission surveillance, but in practice, external control over company-based training proved difficult to achieve. In effect, YTS1 bought employer cooperation by creating a scheme with clear payroll benefits, but minimized the inconvenience by allowing employers to determine training requirements.

During the early stages of the program, MSC guidelines did not require that off-the-job training lead to any externally recognized qualification. Traditionally, the further education (FE) colleges had a monopoly over preparing students for the qualifying examinations for Britain's myriad craft guilds and trade councils. It was, however, relatively expensive for firms to send trainees to courses in the FE colleges. Many companies, especially the larger ones, found it cheaper to provide the required training internally. Because of this, few trainees under YTS1 gained portable credentials. One study found that 76.8 percent of trainees leaving the program between April 1986 and January 1988 received no formal qualification whatsoever.[39] Thus, YTS1 provided low-level work experience with very little training.

Amidst growing concern about the program's inadequacies, the government established the National Council for Vocational Qualifications in 1988 and launched YTS2, which guaranteed 16-year-olds two years of training, increased the minimum duration of off-the-job training to twenty weeks, and placed greater emphasis on occupational competencies in a drive to establish and promote industry-defined standards. The government made it clear that it wanted all YTS2 trainees to complete a recognized formal qualification by the end of their second year.[40] Under YTS2, registration for qualifications increased, and more than half the trainees gained a national vocational qualification (NVQ) certificate.[41]

In 1990, YTS2 was replaced by a third-generation program called simply YT. The new program required employers to bear a greater share of the training costs, and devolved much of the government's regulatory role to local training and enterprise councils (TECs). The objective was to create a structure similar to the private industry councils (PICs) of the United States, thus fostering a greater diversity of local arrangements. Government controls based on inputs, such as the specification of a minimum period of off-the-job training, have been removed or relaxed. Instead control (and increasingly funding) is based on outcomes, which are specified in terms of the competencies defined through the national vocational qualifications.

Because they play key roles in both the training and enterprise councils and industry associations, employers have gained significant influence over the planning and provision of work-based education in Britain. But the system has not been without its critics; even the Confederation of British Industry has questioned the extent to which the standards defined through the NVQs have actually led to improvements in the skills of Britain's young people.[42]

The reform of Britain's training system focused heavily on the importance of standards as an engine of change. With some financial support from the Department of Employment, employers were encouraged to participate in the definition of national vocational qualifications. It was believed that if the definition of the NVQs was in the hands of employers and employer organizations, the right signals would be sent to students and educators, and the standards achieved through both work-based and classroom-based training would improve. However, an analysis of the methods used to develop the NVQs exposes some of the weaknesses of this approach to setting skill standards.

When an NVQ is created, the definition if its content is based mostly on an analysis of the skills required to perform competently in a particular occupation. Analysis leads to the identification of elements of competence, which are "a description of something which a person who works in a given occupational area should be able to do. It is a description of an action, behavior, or outcome which the person should be able to demonstrate."[43] These elements are intended to be evaluated primarily through performance-based assessment, with a priority placed on assessment in workplace contexts. Unfortunately, such an approach often leads to skill definitions that are narrowly focused on the immediate interests of employers, without regard to the general intellectual development of the individual or the longer-term needs of the economy.

This methodology has also resulted in a great deal of variation by sector and occupation in the quality and nature of the NVQs. In some cases, the actions, behaviors, and outcomes specified in an NVQ were grounded in discrete tasks and narrowly defined jobs. Such standards fail to provide young workers with the flexibility they will need to cope with organizational and technological changes in their occupation or even the changes they will face as they move from one employer to another.

The emphasis of the NVQs on workplace assessment arose from an attempt by the government to encourage employers to take greater responsibility for vocational training. The NVQ system expected employers to control the planning, provision, and evaluation of training. But the capacity of employers to deliver training is often limited and varies considerably from one sector of the labor market to another. Under the recessionary conditions that have prevailed since 1990, the amount of employer-provided training has fallen far short of expectations.

In Scotland, despite the increased involvement of employers in YT, much of the most effective training is still taking place in the FE colleges. The courses developed at the colleges have been significantly influenced by the involvement of employers in defining skill requirements, but still, the institutions themselves continue to supply most of the systematic and coordinated training received by Scotland's youth.[44]

A comparison of the experiences of Sweden and Britain suggests that defining standards, publicizing their existence, and providing technical assistance on how they should be used is insufficient to establish an effective training system. There must be a simultaneous focus on setting standards and on developing the capacity of businesses, schools, and colleges to teach the specified skills. Standards provide information to students, teachers, and schools about the knowledge, skills, and attitudes demanded and valued by leading employers. But the standards cannot be achieved without serious investment in curriculum development, teacher training and retraining, and the development of coordinating structures that accredit qualifications and approve alternative providers.

CONCLUSIONS

Employers that participate in school-to-work systems need to provide opportunities for work-based learning, help reform the curricula for vocational and technical courses, and contribute to defining the skills apprentices and trainees are expected to acquire.

In Germany, employers act as senior partners in the training system, and apprentices receive structured training in the workplace. Employers work with unions and educators to define the training curriculum; chambers of industry and commerce monitor the system and conduct the final examinations. Recent developments, however, indicate two disturbing trends. Germany's young people are increasingly choosing academic programs in preference to apprenticeships, creating a shortage of entrants in some occupations. Conversely, in some industries, notably metalworking, the larger companies are finding the expense of apprenticeship training difficult to support, so levels of recruitment are falling. The German apprenticeship system may be less stable than once thought, and it is not clear that it will persist in its traditional form into the twenty-first century.

Britain's struggle to establish a viable system of employment-based youth training illustrates the difficulty of achieving employer compliance in delivering quality training. It also illustrates the folly of relying on skill standards as the driving force for training reform. A high-quality education and training system demands a substantial investment in developing the capacity of schools and training institutions to teach skills.

Both Germany and Sweden provide school-to-work programs for young people 16 to 19 years old on a mass scale. The most radical school-to-work policy proposed for the United States essentially advocates the creation of an American version of the German system. Proponents of this policy envision expanding existing youth apprenticeship programs into a mass system that would provide a structured transition from school to work in a wide range of occupations for a large proportion of U.S. young people.[45] Most youth apprenticeship demonstration programs established in the United States in the past few years operate on a very small scale. These programs show that American employers can deliver small numbers of apprenticeships that are similar to those offered through the German system.[46] It may not, however, be feasible to extend these demonstrations into a mass system. It takes one-quarter of Germany's firms to provide enough apprenticeship places to cover 60 percent of the youth population. At present, the chances of persuading one-quarter of America's employers to participate in a system with this level of intensity seem remote indeed. In Sweden, where the work-based education system imposes fewer demands on employers than in Germany, educators still have difficulties finding enough work placements. And the system of employer associations through which much of this activity is structured is far stronger in Sweden than in the United States.

The British experience casts some light on the limitations of relying on a system of skill standards to improve the quality of youth training in the United States. Despite the absence of any explicit incentives or subsidies in the United States to boost employer participation, some policymakers believe that a widespread system of skill standards will somehow induce employers to participate. The British system of NVQs does seem to have increased the number of employers who have been willing to hire subsidized trainees, but even so, many of these trainees do not receive high-quality training. In Britain it is the educational institutions that still carry most of the training burden.

In the United States, career academies, school-based enterprises, and cooperative education programs illustrate the range of ways in which businesses and schools can share responsibility for providing work experience, setting standards, developing curricula, and mentoring young people. These programs are less intensive than the youth apprenticeship model, but there is some evidence that they can reinvigorate the high school curriculum, reduce dropout rates, and improve student motivation.[47] As Thomas Bailey notes in the introduction, more research is needed to establish an optimum balance between intensity and scale, but if a less intensive model such as the Swedish one (or a carefully extended version of the British approach) could be made to succeed in America, there is reason to be optimistic about the possibility of achieving work-based learning on the desired scale in this country.

NOTES

1. Mari Sako, "The Role of Employers and Unions in Facilitating the Transition to Employment and Further Learning," in Laurel McFarland and Margaret Vickers, eds., *Vocational Education and Training for Youth: Toward Coherent Policy and Practice* (Paris: OECD, 1994). See also Janet Hansen,

Preparing for the Workplace: Charting a Course for Federal Postsecondary Training Policy (Washington: National Academy Press, 1994), p. 105.

2. Antonius Lipsmeier, "The Historical Context of VOTEC in Germany: Major Reforms and Debates," in *The Changing Role of Vocational and Technical Education and Training (VOTEC)* (Institut für Berufspädagogik und Allgemeine Pädagogik, Universität Karlsruhe, 1990).

3. Stephen F. Hamilton, *Apprenticeship for Adulthood: Preparing Youth for the Future* (Free Press, 1990).

4. Ibid.

5. Richard Koch and Jochen Reuling, eds., *Vocational Training in Germany: Modernization and Responsiveness* (Paris: OECD, 1994).

6. Burkart Lutz, "The Difficult Rediscovery of 'Professionality,'" paper presented to the Seminar on Apprenticeship, Alternance and the Dual System: Dead Ends or Highways to the Future, OECD and the Centre d'Etudes de Recherches sur les Qualifications (CEREQ), Marseilles, April 1994.

7. Ibid. The two English words *trade* and *profession* are both translated by the German *Beruf.*

8. Carola Kaps, "Germany's Most Attractive Export Product," *Europe: Magazine of the European Community* (April 1993), pp. 35–36.

9. Koch and Reuling, *Vocational Training in Germany.*

10. Secretariat to the Standing Committee of the Ministers of Education and Cultural Affairs of the Länder, *The Educational System in the Federal Republic of Germany* (Bonn: Foreign Office, 1982), pp. 28–29.

11. Ibid.

12. These differences were discussed in the Integrated Learning Working Group at the OECD-CEREQ seminar (see note 6). See also Margaret Vickers, "Integrated Learning: An Overview of Current Developments in the United States, Britain, and Australia," Expert Group on Integrated Learning, OECD, Paris, 1994.

13. Ibid.

14. Hansen, *Preparing for the Workplace*, p. 105.

15. Secretariat to the Standing Committee, *Educational System in the Federal Republic*, p. 29.

16. Dietmar Harhoff and Thomas Kane, "Financing Apprenticeship Training: Evidence from Germany," Working Paper 4557 (Cambridge, Mass.: National Bureau of Economic Research, December 1993); and Wolfgang Franz and David Soskice, "The German Apprenticeship System," Discussion Paper (Berlin: Social Science Research Center, March 1994).

17. Berndt Söhngen, "The Changing Situation in Germany," paper presented to the Seminar on Employer Participation in School-to-Work Programs, Brookings Institution, Washington, May 4, 1994. Franz and Soskice, "German Apprenticeship System," calculated a net annual cost per apprentice in 1985 of DM 15,000, approximately $5,000.

18. Franz and Soskice, "German Apprenticeship System."

19. Ute Laur-Ernst, "The Dual System in Germany—Advantages of Cooperative Models of Vocational Training," in *Schools and Industry: Partners for a Quality Education: EC/US Conference—The Proceedings* (Noordwijk, Netherlands: Task Force on Human Resources, Education Training and Youth of the Commission of the European Communities, in cooperation with the United States Department of Education, by NUFFIC—Netherlands Organization for International Cooperation in Higher Education, June 1992), p. 30.

20. Information supplied by Siemens-AG to Davis Jenkins, member of the U.S. Competitive Learning Team delegation to Germany, December 1993.

21. "Put Germany Back to Work," *Economist,* October 1993, p. 81.

22. Harhoff and Kane, "Financing Apprenticeship Training."

23. "Put Germany Back to Work," p. 81.

24. Koch and Reuling, *Vocational Training in Germany,* p. 31.

25. For a detailed description, see Secretariat to the Standing Committee, *Educational System in the Federal Republic.*

26. "O Brave New World," *Economist,* March 12, 1994, p. 26.

27. Nicholas Pyke, "Apprentices in Search of a Sorcerer?" *Times Educational Supplement,* July 10, 1992, p. 14.

28. This career pattern is beginning to resemble the American pattern, in which many business schools prefer applicants who have had some serious work experience.

29. Lutz, "Difficult Rediscovery of 'Professionality.'"

30. Statistics Sweden, *Education an Suede* (Orebro, Sweden: SCB Tryckeri, 1993).

31. Swedish National Agency for Education, *The New Upper-Secondary School* (Stockholm: Ministry for Education and Science, 1992).

32. Ibid.

33. Margaret Vickers, interview with Bertil Bucht, deputy assistant under-secretary for secondary and adult education, Ministry of Education, July 1993.

34. Ministry for Education and Science, "Knowledge and Progress: A Summary of the Swedish Government's Bills on Higher Education and Research," Stockholm, February 1993.

35. Margaret Vickers, interview with Anita Ferm, director of upper-secondary education, Local Educational Authority, Gryt, Sweden, July 1993.

36. Margaret Vickers, interview with Åke Lind, director of the Educational and Vocational Training Policy Section, Association of Swedish Engineering Industries, Norrköping, Sweden, July 1993.

37. Margaret Vickers, interview with Anita Ferm, November 1994.

38. Margaret Vickers, interview with Åke Lind, July 1993.

39. H. G. De Ville, *Review of Vocational Qualifications in England and Wales* (London: HMSO, 1986).

40. Manpower Services Commission, Development of the Youth Training

Scheme: A Report (Sheffield, England, 1985).

41. I. S. Jones, "An Evaluation of YTS," *Oxford Review of Economic Policy*, vol. 4 (1988), pp. 54–67.

42. Confederation of British Industry, *Toward a Skills Revolution: A Youth Charter* (London, 1989).

43. Work-Based Learning Project, "Guide to Work-Based Learning Terms, " Bristol, Further Education Staff College, p. 51, details the unevenness by sector in employer-based provision.

44. For a more detailed discussion see Margaret Vickers, "Skill Standards and Skill Formation: Cross-National Perspectives on Alternative Training Strategies," *Jobs for the Future*, Cambridge, Mass., 1994.

45. Richard Kazis, *Improving the Transition from School to Work in the United States* (Washington: American Youth Policy Forum, Competitiveness Policy Council, and Jobs for the Future, 1993). See also *Jobs for the Future, Essential Elements of Youth Apprenticeships Programs: A Preliminary Outline* (Cambridge, Mass., 1991).

46. Stephen F. Hamilton and Mary Agnes Hamilton, "A Progress Report on Apprenticeships," *Educational Leadership*, vol. 49 (March 1992), pp. 44–45; and John Holusha, "The Apprentices' Youthful Tale," *New York Times*, November 1, 1992, p. E26.

47. See the chapter by David Stern in this volume.

Chapter 4

DAVID STERN

Employer Options for Participation in School-to-Work Programs

The transition from school to work for young people in the United States usually takes years. Before they leave high school, most students have already worked in part-time jobs after school and during the summer. Two-thirds of high school graduates continue directly on to postsecondary education, and most hold paid jobs while enrolled. However, students' jobs are seldom related to what they are studying in school or to their desired careers.[1] School and work are separate and sometimes competing activities.

Furthermore, young people tend to work at a job for relatively short periods and often experience unemployment. In some communities, and particularly among African Americans, the rates of youth unemployment and nonemployment are chronically high. Compared with young people in other OECD countries, a large proportion of Americans move from one short-term job to another until they are well into their thirties.[2] Although some mobility can be helpful in finding suitable work, too much takes a toll on career development.

States and localities, now encouraged by the School-to-Work Opportunities Act of 1994 and other federal legislation, are attempting to design new institutional arrangements that will enable more young people to work in a coherent sequence of jobs leading to a stable career. Although the details of these school-to-work programs vary, most share such features as the integration of school-based and work-based learning and a combined academic and vocational curriculum.[3]

The chapters in this book focus on the crucial role of employers in promoting these programs, a role that differentiates school-to-work strategies from other education reforms. The most ambitious models are based on the intensive participation of employers in providing specially designed and coordinated job placements, which many analysts now agree have potentially significant educational benefits.[4] Indeed, whether part-time after school, during the summer, or for entire days or weeks during the school year, these jobs in business and industry are often considered the sine qua non of new school-to-work programs.

The discussion in this book has also emphasized the practical difficulties in developing large numbers of high-quality placements. For example, Margaret Vickers contends that the extensive system of apprenticeship placements in Germany is based on historical, cultural, and institutional traditions missing in the United States. Thomas Bailey argues that there is a trade-off between the intensity and the spread of employer involvement, that the more intense the participation required the more difficult it is to recruit employers to provide job placements.

This chapter explores the variety of roles that employers might assume in an expanded school-to-work system. If there is an inverse relationship between the intensity and spread of work-based education, what are the less intensive options open to employers and how might they help achieve school-to-work program goals?

EFFECTIVE WORK PLACEMENTS

Although large numbers of high school and community college students hold jobs, these jobs sometimes compete with rather than reinforce school-based education.[5] Designers of new school-to-work programs want work-based learning to enhance, not undermine, classroom learning. And, in the longer term, the workplace should provide young people with marketable skills and prepare them for learning throughout their working lives. For these reasons, activities on the job should apply and extend concepts learned in the classroom. Correspondingly, the classroom curriculum should address problems arising from the workplace.

The main attempt so far to create this difficult kind of linkage for U.S. high school students has been cooperative education. An estimated 400,000 high school students each year participate in programs that place them in jobs related to their vocational field of study. In principle, written training plans specify what they are to learn on the job, and their performance is evaluated by teachers in coordination with job supervisors. But research on high school programs indicates that although cooperative education strengthens the connection between school and work in students' minds, students who participate do not generally earn higher incomes after high school than do nonparticipants except for those participants who continue working with their high school employer. In addition, co-op students are less likely than other students to enroll in postsecondary education.[6]

The definition of the work-based learning component in the School-to-Work Opportunities Act specifies that it must include

—work experience;

—a planned program of job training and work experiences coordinated with learning in the school-based component that is relevant to the career majors of students and leads to the awarding of skill certificates;

—workplace mentoring;

—instruction in general workplace competencies, including positive work attitudes and employability and participative skills; and

—broad instruction, to the extent practicable, in all aspects of the industry.

This is a tall order. The requirements for the content of work-based learning for students will present stiff challenges for many businesses that have never offered systematic training even for their regular employees. The challenge is still greater if placements are regarded as ways not only to teach entry-level job skills, but also to deepen students' understanding of their academic subjects. As part of an integrated vocational-academic curriculum, for example, students can be given research and problem-solving assignments to be carried out in the workplace.

Helping students accomplish these learning objectives requires effort by the employer. For example, the Broome County, New York, youth apprenticeship model calls on members of the employer team to fulfill the following responsibilities.

—Provide a training director to manage the company's apprenticeship program. The director works with area coordinators to design apprenticeships and select apprentices, maintain records and evaluate apprentices' progress, serve as a contact with schools and parents, and help train other members of the employer team.

—Provide area coordinators to supervise apprentices in their work areas. Supervision includes determining activities and what can be learned from them, assigning coaches, and serving as a contact with classroom teachers and school counselors.

—Provide coaches to teach apprentices. Coaches are expected to demonstrate and explain tasks, critique performances, and support and encourage apprentices.

—Provide mentors to advise apprentices. This role includes counseling about career directions, initiating apprentices into the culture of the workplace, and serving as another liaison with parents and schools.[7]

The contacts between schools and students and parents are important not only for explaining the nature of the program and dealing with scheduling and other practical issues, but also for helping students learn, especially when something goes wrong. To begin with, some students who are interviewed for an apprenticeship may not be accepted. In the Philadelphia academies program, students who are interviewed and not accepted for summer jobs are told why they were not chosen so that they can try to do better in the next interview rather than feel defeated and give up. Those who are accepted for a job or apprenticeship may still experience failures, of course, and it is vital that programs be structured so that they can learn from their mistakes. Likewise, if a student's substandard performance is somehow attributable to the school, the school staff need to know about it so that they can try to correct what is wrong.

Although decades of experience with cooperative education in this country and observations of programs abroad have enabled observers to describe some critical elements of high-quality work placements, there has been little empirical research relating the characteristics of students' jobs to their subsequent performance in the labor market or postsecondary education. The clearest finding so far from analysis of longitudinal data is that students who report greater opportunities for learning in their high school jobs usually earn higher wages in the first few years after high school.[8] This confirms the importance of carefully designing the work-based component of a school-to-work program so that students really learn something from it.

ALTERNATIVE ROLES FOR EMPLOYERS

Although work-based education in well-designed job placements may be of significant benefit for many young people, poorly designed job placements will provide no more education than do the jobs that so many of them already have. Given the difficulties of recruiting large numbers of employers who are willing to devote the time and resources to developing high-quality placements, it therefore becomes important to consider less demanding alternatives for employer participation that might still preserve some or all of the benefits of the more ambitious involvement. Such alternatives are described in the following pages, arranged into three groups according to the decreasing commitment they require of employers. The alternatives requiring the most involvement entail a change in the operations of the business, but to a lesser extent than providing paid training slots for students. The second set requires a significant commitment of time from employers and workers, but no change in internal operations. The third set calls for only a minimal commitment of time.

Measures Requiring Changes in Internal Business Operations

Providing paid training for students means incorporating them into the company's compensation structure and complying with fair labor standards, child labor laws, health and safety regulations, and other rules covering paid employees. For companies that are reluctant to pay students in work-based learning placements, there are other ways to participate in a school-to-work system. Though less demanding than paid training, these arrangements still place substantial burdens on employers.

Providing job shadowing and unpaid internships. Unpaid job shadowing (following a worker on the job and watching what he or she does), mentoring, and career exploration internships help young students learn enough about various occupations to begin planning their careers. Each of these means of career exploration requires employers to organize certain of their workdays or the workdays of their employees so that they include students in meaningful ways. Because shadowing, mentoring, and career exploration internships may last a year or more, they require a significant commitment from employers and employees to be available to work with students for that long.

Offering placements for teachers. One of the implications of a combined academic-vocational curriculum is that nonvocational teachers must be able to understand and deal with work-related issues. Academic problems and concepts related to the program's career focus must be woven through courses in mathematics, English, science, and social studies. Interdisciplinary projects that let students apply their knowledge from academic disciplines to practical problems related to work also have to be established. But most nonvocational teachers are not equipped to offer this kind of instruction because they lack experience in the relevant field or fields.

Nonvocational teachers need field experience if they are going to share the responsibility for supervising students at the work site. Such responsibilities include helping to write on-the-job training plans, visiting students at work, and evaluating the success of students and programs. As work-based learning becomes a more important part of students' lives in school-to-work programs, the task of supervision will become too large and burdensome for vocational teachers alone, and their academic colleagues will be called on to help.

Employers can assist by offering internships to nonvocational teachers, presumably during the summer. Ideally, the teachers would be given assignments that would make use of their specialized knowledge. For example, mathematics teachers have been hired to help train regular employees in statistical analysis for quality control. In any event, the teachers would have to be paid. Some of their salary might be subsidized by funds designated for teacher training from the School-to-Work Opportunities Act.

Recognizing new skill standards. Within the past few years, serious efforts have begun in the United States to establish skill standards for industries and occupations. As of 1993 the Departments of Labor and Education had contracted with business and industry associations to write new standards for twenty-two industries or occupational groups. The Goals 2000 Act, passed by Congress in March 1994, authorizes a National Skill Standards Board to promote the adoption of standards for clusters of occupations. Additional work on skill standards will take place pursuant to the School-to-Work Opportunities Act.

In the early phases of development, employers have not had to devote large amounts of time to creating standards because trade associations and a few industry representatives are doing most of the work. But the implementation phase will be different. If standards are to mean anything, at least a substantial minority of companies that conduct training will have to follow them. This will involve a major effort.

The effect of skill standards will depend on how many employers will give some kind of preferential treatment to job applicants who have been certified. This is an essential feature of traditional apprenticeships both in the United States and abroad. The evidence on high school cooperative education in this country—that it results in higher earnings only if students remain employed with their program employer—indicates what happens in the absence of recognized and valued certification.

Encouraging student attendance and performance. Because many students already work, employers have opportunities to relate students' paid employment to what they are learning in school and to encourage school attendance and academic effort. Employers can become involved through such simple strategies as asking potential student employees for the most recent record of their grades in school and their record of attendance. The message to students would be clear: how well they do in school and how good their attendance is, are important to employers. Employers could also ask student workers to submit subsequent reports of grades and attendance to see if there is any drop in performance and attendance that might be attributed in some way to conflicting demands of work and school.

Measures Requiring Commitment of Time

Employers can support school-to-work efforts without inviting students to the workplace or altering their own internal operations. However, these forms of involvement may still require significant commitments of time.

Counseling individual students. Traditional school-business partnerships have often included efforts by employers to find mentors and counselors for students among their employees. Mentors and students meet outside class time, perhaps at the mentor's workplace, perhaps at a restaurant for lunch. They may attend special events together at the workplace or at school. The mentor can become a role model, talking with a student about the nature of the career field, the connection with school, preparing for a job interview, or plans for future work and further education. These interactions expand students' ideas of work and increase the number of adults with whom they come into contact, helping them understand how adults behave at work and what is expected of them.

Providing instruction and field trips. Representatives of local employers may also provide direct instruction to students. As guest speakers in classes, they can supply specialized information and create a personal connection between the classroom and the world of work that boosts the school's legitimacy in students' eyes. Employers can also host field trips to workplaces. Such trips give students a better understanding of the work being performed there and of the various occupations involved in a particular business or industry. And visits to offices, laboratories, and manufacturing facilities also let them bridge a social gap that many of them would not otherwise be able to cross. Thus, like the activities of mentors, classroom presentations and field trips help students gain a better understanding of the adult world of work than traditional schooling can provide.

Giving advice on curriculum, instruction, and assessment. Employers often contribute their advice and perspectives on school activities, programs, and goals. They may serve as members of school boards and school-based management committees. There is a long history of employer involvement in vocational education through participation on advisory and craft committees. These committees help schools become aware of work requirements and industry standards. Educators can use this information to design curricula, instructional materials, and assessment guidelines.

Beyond assuming an advisory role, employers can become active participants in designing new curricula. They have assisted local schools to develop programs in health occupations, electronics, computer-related occupations, finance, and many other fields. As more programs demand these specialized, work-oriented curricula, there will be economies of scale that justify greater efforts at the regional and national levels, but even the best lesson plans must be modified for local use. Modification can be a demanding activity because it may require local employers to become involved in the details of curriculum development. They have to become acquainted with local and state requirements for high school graduation and familiar with college admission requirements if they are to help teachers find work-related applications of academic subject matter. Employers might be particularly helpful in putting together interdisciplinary projects and weaving courses together so that they approach similar work-related concepts from different perspectives. And once such a curriculum is in place, of course, it must be continually modified to accommodate changes in the work context and in local circumstances.

Although this process may be difficult and time consuming, it does produce results, and it may be especially feasible for representatives of employer organizations, as illustrated by Margaret Vickers in her description of developments in Sweden. Staff members of employer organizations, who often have backgrounds in business and industry, may have more time and resources than individual employers to develop the expertise required to participate in curriculum development.

Donating Money or Materials

Without providing paid training, altering their internal operations, or spending significant amounts of time, employers can still contribute by donating money, equipment, and materials to schools, which, in an era of severe pressures on school budgets, is much to be welcomed. Businesses may provide relatively up-to-date equipment for training students in the schools' laboratories and workshops, purchase fax machines or telephone answering machines to help schools keep in touch with job placements, or cover the cost of travel or other expenses not included in school budgets. This type of involvement requires little time, but the financial contributions can be substantial. Businesses associated with the Philadelphia high school academies in 1992 contributed $1.2 million in cash, or about $400 for each academy student.

THE OPTION OF SCHOOL-BASED WORK EXPERIENCE

Although much of the recent discussion of improving school-to-work transition has focused on placing high school students as trainees in business and industry, greater use could be made of work experience organized by the school itself. A 1992 survey estimated that 18.6 percent of secondary schools sponsored programs in which students build houses, run restaurants, staff child care centers, repair cars, manage retail stores, or produce other goods and services.[9] Like teaching hospitals associated with medical schools or law review journals written by law students, most school-based enterprises at the secondary level are part of vocational education. However, there are enterprises attached to nonvocational classes, and those that have begun as part of vocational education could be extended to accompany a combined academic-vocational curriculum.

Unlike students working in cooperative education programs, in which they are usually paid, those working in these enterprises usually are not. However, students who work in school-based enterprises and also hold paid jobs not connected with school report that the school-based work experience has greater educational value. School-based enterprises give them more opportunity to apply what they have learned in their classes and to learn new things.[10]

Providing work experience in school-based enterprises demands less time and effort from outside employers than if they provide it themselves, although local businesses are still called on to contribute advice, equipment, and other assistance. Sometimes there is a quid pro quo. Mount Edgecumbe High School in Sitka, Alaska, for example, has created a product development laboratory for local fish processors: they provide the raw material, and students test new methods of processing and packaging for commercial sale.[11] Employers can also learn from some school-based enterprises about how best to organize work to facilitate learning, an increasingly important strategy for companies faced with fast-changing technologies and product markets.

However, existing school-based enterprises cannot provide work experience for large numbers of students. Although numerous, they are small. Expanding them to accommodate more than the 100,000 or so students who now participate each year would be a large task. And competition with local businesses, always a delicate issue, would become more serious if school-based enterprises expanded significantly. The number of teachers who are capable of running such an enterprise is also limited, and more would have to be trained. New curricula would have to be designed, new schedules created, and new routines developed if work-based learning is to become a more integral part of high schools, whether in school enterprises or in workplaces outside the school.

CONCLUSION

In this country, schools have primary responsibility for educating and training most young people. Under a German-style dual system, employers would take over at age 16 or 17, but U.S. employers have not yet indicated that they want this responsibility. Therefore, their role has mainly been limited to assisting the schools. But collaborating with schools to create a new school-to-work system will itself demand a great deal of time and effort. It remains to be seen how much will be forthcoming. In the meantime, schools can increase their current capacity to provide work-based learning under their own auspices.

NOTES

1. James R. Stone and others, "Adolescents' Perceptions of Their Work: School Supervised and Non-School Supervised," *Journal of Vocational Education Research,* vol. 15 (Spring 1990), pp. 31–53.

2. Organization for Economic Cooperation and Development, *Employment Outlook* (July 1993), tables 4.3, 4.4.

3. See the introduction for a further discussion of the labor market and educational problems that underlie the school-to-work transition movement and an analysis of the characteristics of school-to-work programs.

4. See, for example, Stephen F. Hamilton, *Apprenticeship for Adulthood: Preparing Youth for the Future* (Free Press, 1990).

5. Lawrence D. Steinberg, Suzanne Fegley, and Sanford M. Dornbusch, "Negative Impact of Part-Time Work on Adolescent Adjustment: Evidence from a Longitudinal Study," *Developmental Psychology,* vol. 29 (March 1993), pp. 170–80.

6. David Stern and others, *School to Work: Research on Programs in the United States* (Bristol, Pa.: Taylor and Francis Falmer Press, 1995), pp. 20, 21, 48, 52.

7. Stephen F. Hamilton, Mary Agnes Hamilton, and Benjamin J. Wood, *Creating Apprenticeship Opportunities for Youth,* a progress report from the Youth Apprenticeship Demonstration Project in Broome County, New York, Cornell University, September 1991.

8. David Stern and others, *School to Work,* p. 51.

9. David Stern and others, *School-Based Enterprise: Productive Learning in American High Schools* (San Francisco: Jossey-Bass, 1994), p. 5.

10. Stern and others, *School-Based Enterprise,* pp. 11–15.

11. Stern and others, *School-Based Enterprise,* p. 95.

Chapter 5

ROBERT POCZIK

Work-Based Education and School Reform

It has long been held that people learn best when they learn skills in the context in which the information is used.[1] Work-based education, a special variant of this concept, can provide a focus for academic learning and significantly influence young people's intellectual development by enabling them to learn about a range of jobs and careers, experience the daily work of adults engaged in various occupations, and prepare themselves to enter an occupation or career field.[2] For these reasons, work-based education became a cornerstone of the School-to-Work Opportunities Act of 1994.

But work-based education programs can yield these benefits only in conjunction with significant reforms in the ways schools and schooling are structured. If the programs are merely grafted onto traditional structures, they will be of little value. Indeed, in such a case the programs could be considered not only of marginal use but as competing with school-based academic learning. If schools are to have any chance of developing the job placements and related interactions with employers that an effective school-to-work system requires, they will have to make significant changes in scheduling and other activities.

WHY SCHOOLS MUST CHANGE

Effective work-based education will require significant school restructuring because such programs involve much more than students' simply spending time on a job. After all, most high school students already have jobs, and working during high school can actually impair school performance.[3] Cooperative education programs, which are less structured and intensive than work-based education as it is envisioned in the School-to-Work Opportunities Act, increase subsequent wages only when the students stay on with the employer who provided their placement.[4] Thus although the students participating in co-op programs may learn skills that are useful for the employer who provides the placement, cooperative education provides no documented advantage in acquiring skills that would be more generally useful in the labor market.

To improve students' academic skills, work-based education must be explicitly related to the learning taking place in the classroom and must lead to a recognized credential.[5] The German apprenticeship system, for example, meets both criteria.[6] For this reason, the School-to-Work Opportunities Act requires that schools offer "a planned program of job training and work experiences (including training related to preemployment and employment skills to be mastered at progressively higher levels) that are coordinated with the school-based learning component . . . and lead to the award of skills certificates." The act also emphasizes the need for mechanisms that link school-based and work-based education and link employers with schools.

To attract a large number of young people, work-based education must be appropriate both for students who will proceed directly to work after high school and those who will immediately pursue postsecondary education. In the United States nine out of ten twelfth graders expect to continue their education beyond high school, with half planning to enroll immediately in a four-year college or university.[7] Educational programs that preclude college preparation tend to become second-class activities avoided by parents and students who wish to keep options open. If work is to become an integral part of high school programs for large numbers of college-bound students, it must be structured in such a way that it does not compete with the perceived real work of high schools to prepare students for college. If students are to be placed in work sites to engage in work-based education, what academic knowledge and skills can be acquired or reinforced there? How can courses be structured so that school-based learning can take place in fewer classroom hours? How can students' jobs outside school hours be made a part of their total instructional program, or will those in work-based education simply be expected to put in longer hours? These questions reflect the magnitude of the changes that will have to take place in schools if work-based education is to move beyond marginal add-on programs serving small numbers of students.

School-to-work strategies and associated work-based education must become an integral part of new approaches to curricula, instruction, and assessment. These developments could support and be complementary to work-based programs, but if they are considered separate reforms, they could compete with the programs for time, attention, and resources.

Finally, the implementation of the School-to-Work Opportunities Act requires the development of partnerships between schools and outside supporters at the national, state, and local levels. Principal among these partners will be leaders in business and labor. In the past, schools have had limited interaction with employers and labor unions and certainly have not had the type of intensive partnership necessary to develop and make high-quality, work-based programs available to large numbers of students. Employers seem willing to engage in such partnerships.[8] It may, however, prove difficult for schools to include them fully in planning for and implementing the relevant school restructuring.

WHAT IS WORK-BASED EDUCATION?

Work-based education is defined somewhat narrowly in the School-to-Work Opportunities Act as a program that prepares students for work in a particular occupation or field and includes work experience, preferably for pay. As I use the term, work-based education is learning related to work and careers, and the workplace provides the opportunity to apply the learning. In this sense the concept can be integrated with any subject, academic or vocational, in the school curriculum and can encourage career awareness, exploration, and planning as well as help students prepare for a particular occupation or field. The work experience can be paid or unpaid and can occur at work sites or school sites, as in the case of school-based enterprises.

Work-based programs can serve a number of purposes in the education of young people. First, these programs pay more serious attention than do academic programs to exposing students to the various workplaces and kinds of work that take place in a community. This effort can build on efforts in elementary schools to invite parents and other members of the community to come into the classroom to tell about the work they do and to take children on field trips to local work sites. But efforts to encourage career awareness under a comprehensive approach to school-to-work will be more formal and will be developed over a multiyear period. Several commercially available programs, including Junior Achievement and Kids and the Power of Work (KAPOW), provide resources to elementary teachers for this purpose.

Building on their exposure as elementary students, middle school students can begin purposefully to explore fields of interest, perhaps through job shadowing, in which a student accompanies a worker on typical duties, and mentoring. This career exploration is to lay the foundation for students, parents, teachers, counselors, and mentors to collaborate in creating students' initial career plans. These plans, which students will be expected to revisit and revise during their high school studies, will begin to influence their choices of what they will study in school, the kinds of work experiences they will engage in, and the kinds of employment and further studies they will pursue after high school. The career development guidelines issued by the National Occupational Information Coordinating Committee and the companion career development portfolio provide a structure and resources to guide this process.[9]

All students will be expected to acquire workplace competencies that underlie successful performance in a range of occupations. These competencies, which have been fully outlined by the Secretary's Commission on Achieving Necessary Skills (SCANS), include basic and advanced communications skills, as well as thinking, decision-making, resource management, and teamwork.[10] Instruction in these skills is to be built into school curricula beginning in the elementary grades. Although they can be taught and practiced in school settings, they can be most effectively mastered in workplaces. Various ways of assessing the acquisition of these basics have been devised, including the Work Keys assessment instruments being developed by American College Testing. These basics are also one of the bases of the certificates of initial mastery called for by the Commission on the Skills of the American Workforce.[11]

All students, regardless of which career they choose to follow and whether they will go directly to work after high school or pursue further studies, should be expected to meet certain common academic standards. These standards are being defined in many states through school reform efforts. Higher academic standards can be expected to be given impetus through the Goals 2000 plans being developed by all states. Schools will need to be certain that work-based education opportunities encourage and enable students to acquire the skills required of all students for graduation from high school. In this sense, all students would acquire and demonstrate the same kinds of skills, only in different contexts. Work-based education has the potential to enable underachieving students to acquire higher levels of knowledge, skills, and competencies than they ordinarily might because they would learn and use them in meaningful contexts. Tech-prep education programs have developed considerable expertise in applied academics, and high-quality curricula in applied mathematics, science, communication, and economics are available nationally.[12]

When students are ready to prepare seriously for an occupation or career, schools, colleges, and employers in partnership need to make available career or occupationally specific programs. These programs should include classwork, supervised work experiences or internships related to the classwork, building a resume or portfolio, awarding diplomas, degrees, and certificates, and assistance with transition from school to work. It is in these programs that the certificates of advanced mastery described in *America's Choice* become a mark of having achieved skill levels that meet industry standards. What may distinguish such programs from ones currently available through vocational education is that they are likely to be broader and less job specific. In the future they may also be organized around career majors, as called for by the School-to-Work Opportunities Act. It is here that efforts to define national skills standards and criteria for skills certificates will be important. The development of these standards will gather speed with the establishment of the National Skills Standards Board under Goals 2000: Educate America Act.

EMPLOYER INVOLVEMENT IN WORK-BASED EDUCATION

Work-based education can become an integral part of learning for all students only with a significant commitment of time and effort on the part of employers. The student, a teacher or advisor, the parents of the student, and the employer must together develop a work experience plan. Employers agree to provide supervision of students at the work site and may be asked to help assess their performance. Cooperative education programs are the most common form of school-sponsored work experiences, with youth apprenticeships growing in importance as an option. Labor unions must be involved in the design and operation of apprenticeships.

This chapter discusses the types of school-based changes necessary to facilitate this significant commitment on the part of employers. Nevertheless, a range of less demanding or intensive forms of involvement can be made available to employers who are reluctant to provide fully developed work placements. These alternatives, discussed in more detail in the chapter by David Stern, include giving advice regarding curricula, instruction, and assessment; providing guest speakers and site visits; providing job shadowing, mentoring, and career internship opportunities; and encouraging good school attendance and performance. By offering employers a variety of options for working with students, schools increase the likelihood that a wider range and larger number of employers will become engaged in some form of work-based education and in related school restructuring.

RESTRUCTURING SCHOOLS

Work-based education has much to offer students but will require a considerable commitment from educators working in conjunction with employers, parents, and students to develop the programs as an integral part of every young person's education. Many barriers will be encountered, and surmounting them will require a restructuring of schools.

Commitment of School Administrators

Superintendents and principals must support work-based education if it is to become an integral part of the school program. Full implementation will require extra time and effort on the part of school personnel. It will demand flexibility in the school schedule and will raise questions of health, safety, and liability regarding students at work sites. Superintendents and principals will be more likely to support the program if it is promoted by business leaders in the community and supported by parents. Superintendents and principals are also more likely to give support if the program clearly encourages young people to remain in school and earn a high school diploma, and if it can be shown to strengthen academic performance through rigorous applied learning.

Commitment and Preparation of Teachers

Gaining the support and involvement of teachers is also essential, but it faces some obstacles, not the least of which is a certain cynicism toward new movements in education. It will be difficult to get teachers to believe that work-based education can be an effective core instructional strategy and can become a permanent part of the education system. To convince them, national and state policymakers must provide consistent leadership and resources over a period of years so that the innovation can become institutionalized.

Even if teachers become interested in developing work-based education, they will need to deal with an already overcrowded curriculum and school schedule, and the pressure to prepare students to succeed on required examinations. They will need workable strategies they can use to incorporate the new program into existing courses. They will also need time to visit work sites to understand current and emerging patterns of work and skill requirements, to develop curricula and instructional strategies to connect work-based education with knowledge and skills taught in traditional academic subjects, to visit students at work sites, and to review student projects and journals. Teachers will discover that cooperative learning, interdisciplinary teaching, team teaching, and performance-based learning and assessment are well suited to work-based education. But it will be essential to provide them with time and resources to secure their involvement. This sort of teacher support would constitute a valuable use of venture capital to be made available to states and localities under the School-to-Work Opportunities Act.

Availability and Preparation of Counselors

Career awareness, exploration, and planning help students make choices regarding work-based education experiences. School counselors can be instrumental in providing such career guidance. But there are too few certified counselors, and much of their time is occupied helping students draw up course schedules, manage personal and family crises, and select colleges and prepare college applications. Given the unlikelihood of sharply increasing the number of counselors, strategies need to be worked out for them to engage teachers, employers, workplace mentors, and parents in providing career development opportunities to students. The key to this effort will be enabling counselors to spend time with employers and in work settings to understand current and emerging patterns of work and workplace requirements.

Student Interest and Participation

Even if administrators, teachers, and counselors were committed to offering work-based education opportunities, the effort would be of little value if students did not avail themselves of them. High school students, particularly juniors and seniors, have many demands on their schedules from homework, extracurricular activities, and paid work. If work-based education simply seems something to add to an already overburdened schedule, they will not want to participate. If, however, work experiences are woven into regular school courses and count as credit toward course completion, they will seem less an add-on. And if work experiences add interest to regular school subjects, they will seem less a burden. If such experiences could also contribute to a resume that would make a student more attractive to future employers and postsecondary educational institutions, the program would assume even more value.

A recent national survey of fourteen- to eighteen-year-olds indicates that there may be a good deal of latent interest in work-based education.[13] Ninety-five percent said they would be interested in a new program in which they could "learn both in school and on a job." Eighty-nine percent said school would be more interesting if academic courses were taught around careers in which they were interested, and 67 percent said school would be more interesting if part of learning could be done at work.

Parent Interest and Participation

If large numbers of students are to participate in work-based education, parents must also believe that such programs will open up valuable career and college options for them. If the programs are seen as contributing to school performance rather than detracting from it, parents are more likely to support participation. To encourage such support, parents will need to be fully briefed about these learning opportunities before they are widely implemented. School personnel will have to assure them that students will be supervised and safe in work settings. Parents should also be invited to visit work settings with their children to determine if an experience in that setting would be appropriate. And they should be invited to be present when students make reports and presentations on their experiences. This level of parental involvement, however, may prove difficult to realize; nearly half of the nation's students have parents who participate in virtually no school functions.[14]

Employer Participation

Any school district or school attempting to develop work-based education will have to consider what will motivate employers to participate. Experience indicates that they will be more likely to support the programs if they have been involved in designing them. Thus employers should be included early in the development of a program. But because even with early involvement, they will be pressured by the daily demands of their work and the marketplace, schools must routinize their participation by preparing guidelines that will make it easy for them to know what will be expected of them. Such preparation will make it more likely that employers will feel at ease with students engaged in the program. Employers will also need to be provided accurate information on health, safety, and liability matters so that they will not hesitate to participate for fear of inadvertently violating laws. If these barriers can be surmounted, they will see benefits to their participation.[15]

Availability and Preparation of Work-Site Mentors

To be adequately supervised at work sites and for the work to offer them a legitimate learning experience, each student will need to have an assigned work-site mentor. This will require a commitment of time from the mentor that will have to be taken into account when an employer agrees to take on a student. Because the art of mentoring in the workplace, as traditionally carried out through apprenticeships, is not as widespread as it once was, a mentor will need to be briefed on the subjects the student is taking in school, so that he or she can reinforce that academic learning in the student's work experience. If the school creates projects for students to carry out as part of their work experience, the mentor may be asked to advise the student on the project or participate in assessing its quality when completed. Mentors will also need to be provided special assistance if they are assigned a student who has a disability or limited proficiency in English or some other barrier to participation and success. There is some evidence, based on the experience of youth apprenticeship programs, that mentors find working with students to be energizing and personally rewarding.[16]

Ensuring Quality and Connections

Work-based education experiences must be high quality and have a rigor equal to that in other parts of a student's program of learning. This is true both for short-term experiences such as job shadowing and for longer-term internships, cooperative education experiences, and apprenticeships. For longer-term experiences, an individualized work experience plan should be drawn up and signed by representatives of the school and the workplace as well as by the student and his or her parents or guardians. This plan would spell out the nature of the work experience, the location and hours, the responsibilities of the employer and the student, and any school-related assignment or project to be carried out during the work, including keeping a journal. A school-based mentor will also be necessary. In most cases the mentor will be one of the student's teachers, although the role might be assumed by a work-experience coordinator. Cooperative education programs have well-established procedures for designing and supervising school-related work experiences for students enrolled in vocational education programs. These procedures can be modified for use by larger numbers of students in less occupationally specific work-based education experiences.

Assessing and Giving Credit

If work-based education experiences are to be an integral part of a student's program of learning, they should be assessed and students given credit when the requirements have been met. Usually students will be required to demonstrate that they have acquired certain knowledge and skills from the experience and that they have successfully completed whatever assignment or project is required. Judgments regarding the acquisition of skills and the completeness, accuracy, and quality of the work carried out should involve both the work-site mentor and the school-based mentor. Joint assessments help create a closer relationship between the workplace and the school. Schools that require student exhibitions and portfolios for graduation can incorporate the results of the work experience in the portfolios. New York State's school reform efforts emphasize such student projects.[17]

Modifying the School Schedule

Scheduling large numbers of students in a variety of courses is part of the business of operating a high school. But scheduling students to spend part of their day or week in an area vocational center or a work setting can pose special difficulties for both schools and students. Students will need flexibility in their schedules.[18] Scheduling can be handled completely on an individual basis, or certain blocks of time in the school day and week can be set aside for work experiences for all students. Individualized scheduling makes it easier to work around the schedules of employers. Group scheduling makes it easier for larger numbers of students to engage in work experiences. Whatever the option chosen, scheduling must be tackled early in the process of restructuring or else the work experiences will not engage large numbers of students as called for in the School-to-Work Opportunities Act.

Handling the Logistics

Beyond scheduling work during the school day, week, and year, schools will need to maintain a directory of employers willing to engage in the program at some level. This directory could include guest speakers, work-site visits, mentors, job shadowing opportunities, paid and unpaid internships, clinical experiences, cooperative education, and youth apprenticeships. The directory will need to be computerized to keep track of and regularly update a large number of opportunities. The Walks-of-Life program, operated by the Greater New York Hospital Foundation, has developed just such a computer program. The whereabouts of students participating in one or another of the forms of work-based education on any given day will need to be tracked so that they are accounted for at all times.

Transportation to and from work sites also needs to be arranged. Arrangements will vary greatly depending on whether the school is in an urban area where public transportation is readily available or in a suburban or rural area where it may be more limited. If transportation is limited, school buses may be needed, in which case block scheduling of students will probably be necessary. An additional consideration is whether large numbers of students drive cars to school and can drive to and from work sites. Area vocational centers and cooperative education programs have a great deal of experience with transporting vocational education students to work sites; this experience can be drawn upon by schools to devise means of transporting larger numbers of students to work-based education experiences.

Child Labor Laws and Health, Safety, and Liability Issues

Schools, employers, and parents all will have concerns regarding health, safety, and liability issues related to students' participating in work-based experiences at nonschool sites. Schools will want to ensure that the work site has been visited by school staff so that they can assure parents of its safety and appropriateness. Schools will also need to know where all students are at any given time. Employers will want to know the extent of their responsibility for students and their liability. School personnel need to be aware of sexual harassment in the workplace and either modify the work-site arrangements or remove the student from the site should such harassment continue.

Liability for students is clear enough when they are paid, but becomes much less clear when they are engaged in unpaid work related to career exploration.[19] Local, state, and regional Department of Labor offices, in conjunction with employer and labor organizations, can help address and resolve liability issues and others related to child labor laws. The AFL-CIO Human Resources Development Institute, for example, has issued a publication to help students become aware of their rights as workers under federal law.[20] Unless these health, safety, and liability issues are recognized and dealt with, it is unlikely that large numbers of students and employers will participate in work-based education experiences.

Work-Based Education and Broader School Reform

Work-based education and school-to-work efforts can have a much greater impact if they are part of broader school reform efforts.[21] Indeed, some current reforms may thwart efforts to develop work-based education if common cause is not made between the different groups of reformers.

A number of state-sponsored reform efforts support shared decisionmaking at the school level as well as stronger local or even site-based control. New York State's New Compact for Learning is a state reform effort that emphasizes stronger local control of decisions regarding teaching and learning in schools.[22] It is not always clear, however, that employers in a community are involved in decisionmaking at the school level. This involvement could have a very beneficial effect on their participation in work-based education.

As local decisionmakers, parents and teachers may consider work a diversion from more important academic pursuits and the program as a threat or a disruption to what they think are superior pedagogic approaches. To the extent that parents and teachers have greater influence, it is particularly important they be convinced that work-based education is effective.

Many state reform efforts place great emphasis on the results to be achieved by students and strive for higher educational standards and greater accountability. There is the potential in these efforts either to reinforce the development of work-based education or stand in its way. If standards include assessments of the skills students learn on the job, the development of the program will be encouraged. But assessments oriented to measuring the outcomes of traditional educational approaches could make the development of a work-based strategy more difficult.

The "authentic assessment" movement, which urges that students demonstrate skills in real-life settings rather than through multiple-choice exams and similar classroom exercises, has the potential to be particularly important in the development of work-based education. Well-designed programs could help students gain experiences working on complex group problem-solving efforts that form the basis of some approaches to authentic assessment. But time spent on the job can easily be seen as a diversion from preparation for written exams and other more traditional assessments.

Many academic disciplines are now developing their own curriculum reform movements. Work-based education will probably thrive best in an interdisciplinary environment. Thus to the extent that the new curricula maintain the divisions between the disciplines, their development will complicate efforts to increase the use of work-based education. But it is possible to develop approaches to curricula, such as the integration of mathematics, science, and technology education, that can encourage it. Thus work-based education proponents must become involved in the broader efforts to reform educational content and methods.

The Goals 2000: Educate America Act gives form and support from the federal government to school reform efforts. It calls on states to set expected levels of student achievement that reflect the national education goals it sets forth. It also requires states to establish and involve citizen panels to develop action plans for school improvement. An opportunity for connecting work-based education with school reform is created by the requirement that there be coordination with school-to-work programs, including work-based education. It will be important for employers to be actively engaged in state-level panels and for work-based education to become a part of state school reform efforts by being a component of school improvement plans under Goals 2000.

STRUCTURAL BARRIERS TO IMPLEMENTING WORK-BASED EDUCATION

This chapter has outlined school reforms that can provide a basis for the development of work-based education. But even if many teachers, principals, and parents agree with these proposals and would like to see them implemented, important barriers remain.

—With 80 percent of eleventh and twelfth grade students working for pay outside school, and with the demands of homework, extracurricular activities, family and community responsibilities, and social life, it will be difficult to get students to commit time to participate in work-based education.

—Most high schools have highly structured bureaucratic organizations with large numbers of students scheduled into a complicated array of course offerings. Any learning activity such as work-based education that requires flexibility conflicts with the schools' need to regularize their schedule of operations.

—Schools tend to undervalue less academically inclined students and to reward students who function well under traditional classroom instruction. Schools do not offer varied learning experiences and options that might appeal to students who do not succeed in the predominant mode of learning. There is also a deeply ingrained sense among academic educators that work-related, applied learning will water down the rigor of the academic curriculum.

—School reform movements often take a long time to develop to the stage at which they actually have much effect on daily teaching and learning. Many are abandoned before they come to fruition. The career education movement of the 1960s, which emphasized infusing students with career awareness as early as the elementary grades, is an example of a reform that was abandoned before it could affect the nature of education.

—In the demanding and highly competitive economic environment in which most businesses operate, it is difficult for employers to commit resources to educate the future workforce. This is especially true of small businesses, in which most students will hold their initial jobs after leaving school. Besides, many employers believe they already have an ample choice of well-educated workers because of the continuing fluidity of the labor market.

—In many areas of the country, especially urban and rural areas, high rates of business failures, unemployment, and poverty make it difficult for students to find jobs. In such areas, employers, workers, and labor unions are likely to be concerned about students taking work away from adults.

STRATEGIES FOR OVERCOMING STRUCTURAL BARRIERS

The six strategies for overcoming structural barriers that are outlined in this section do not have a one-to-one correlation to the six barriers described in the preceding section. Rather, they constitute elements of a coherent strategy on the part of national, state, and local partners to restructure schools and enlist support from educators, employers, unions, parents, and students, so that work-based education opportunities can be made available to all young people.

—National, state, and local partners must make a concerted multi-year effort to restructure the educational system to integrate work-based education into the education of all young persons. The necessary groundwork will in some cases require changes in federal and state legislation to integrate various programs that together can make work-based education widely available. Chief among these programs are vocational education, supported by the Carl D. Perkins Vocational and Applied Technology Education Act, and employment and training programs supported by the Job Training Partnership Act. Integrating them to make certain long-term change actually occurs in schools will require transcending the vagaries of presidential and gubernatorial elections and administrations.[23]

—There need to be efforts at the federal, state, and local levels to connect school reform being carried out under the Goals 2000: Educate America Act with work-based education and other school-to-work efforts. To do this, the efforts of the National Education Standards and Improvement Council, which will address academic standards, and the National Skill Standards Board, which will address occupational skill standards, must be coordinated. If these two bodies, to be established under Goals 2000, are allowed to proceed down separate paths, they will perpetuate the artificial distinction between academic learning and work-related learning, making it difficult for schools to view work-based education as a strategy that can support both academic and workforce preparation. A strong involvement of employers in the council and the board would make it more likely that their efforts would underwrite high standards for both academic learning and workforce preparation.

—A coalition of federal and state Labor Department officials, employer organizations, and labor unions needs to be formed to deal with issues involving child labor laws as well as health, safety, civil rights, and liability related to work-based education. The coalition would work out resolutions to potential problems and communicate them to employers, unions, and schools. Such concerted action would help ensure that these matters do not derail efforts to establish work-based education in all schools.

—Employer organizations at the national, state, and local levels need to work in concert to encourage the employer involvement that will be needed for work-based education to become available to all students. Employer-to-employer communication, promotion, and enlistment must be emphasized to realize the goal of having all employers in every community involved in some form of work-based program.

—To prevent employers from being approached by dozens of persons wanting to enlist them in programs, recruitment will need to be organized on a regional basis. Clearinghouses can be made a part of each state's implementation of the School-to-Work Opportunities Act. States could then make the clearinghouses a required feature of school-to-work efforts at the local level through the local partnerships to be established under the act.

— A major public outreach campaign will be needed to enlist school personnel, students, parents, employers, and unions in broad implementation of work-based education. This outreach effort will need to take place at the national, state, and local levels and will need to involve both public and private partners. Research into public perceptions of work-based education and school-to-work efforts will be needed to design the outreach campaign. For example, educators and parents are concerned about relegating students to vocational and nonvocational tracks. A way of speaking to parents and school personnel about work-based education will have to be devised that does not raise concerns about tracking.[24]

CONCLUSION

For work-based education to be made available to many students on a regular basis, schools must be restructured so that the program becomes an integral part of school reform. To carry out this restructuring, schools and employers must develop long-term partnerships at the national, state and local levels. The School-to-Work Opportunities Act and the Goals 2000: Educate America Act offer opportunities for schools and employers to work together. There is already widespread activity at the state level to restructure schools so that work-based education becomes a valuable part of every young person's education. This activity needs to be encouraged and supported.

NOTES

1. John Dewey, *Experience and Education* (Collier, 1938; reprinted 1963); and Sue Berryman and Thomas Bailey, *The Double Helix of Education and the Economy* (Institute on Education and the Economy, Columbia University, 1992).

2. See, for example, Commission on the Skills of the American Workforce, *America's Choice: High Skills or Low Wages* (Rochester, N.Y.: National Center on

Education and the Economy, 1990).

3. Department of Education, Office of Research, *School to Work: What Does Research Say About It?* (1994); and Stephen F. Hamilton, *Apprenticeship for Adulthood: Preparing Youth for the Future* (Free Press, 1990).

4. David Stern and others, *Research on School-to-Work Transition Programs in the United States* (Berkeley, Calif.: National Center for Research in Vocational Education, 1994).

5. Roy Peters, Jr., *Vocational Education's Role in the Reform Movement in the United States* (The Hague: Netherlands Organization for International Cooperation in Higher Education, 1992); and Dan Hull, *Opening Minds, Opening Doors: The Rebirth of American Education* (Waco, Tex.: CORD Communications, 1993).

6. Hamilton, *Apprenticeship for Adulthood.*

7. Department of Education, *School to Work.*

8. National Alliance of Business, *How School-to-Work Works for Business* (Annapolis, Md.: National Alliance of Business, 1994).

9. American School Counselor Association, "Career Development Portfolio" (Washington: National Occupational Information Coordinating Committee, 1994); and "National Career Development Guidelines" (Washington: National Occupational Information Coordinating Committee, 1992).

10. Secretary's Commission on Achieving Necessary Skills, *What Work Requires of Schools: A SCANS Report for America 2000* (Department of Labor, 1991).

11. See *America's Choice: High Skills or Low Wages.*

12. Hull, *Opening Minds, Opening Doors.*

13. Brushkin Goldring Research, "High School Students Support School-to-Work," Department of Education, 1994.

14. Nicholas Zill and Christine Winquist, "Running in Place," Washington, Child Trends, 1994.

15. National Alliance of Business, *How School-to-Work Works for Business.*

16. Ibid.

17. New York State Education Department, *Learning-Centered Curriculum and Assessment for New York State: Report of the New York State Curriculum and Assessment Council to the Commissioner of Education and the Board of Regents* (Albany, N.Y., 1994).

18. General Accounting Office, *Transition from School-to-Work: States Are Developing New Strategies to Prepare Students for Jobs* (1993).

19. Ibid.

20. AFL-CIO Human Resources Development Institute, "It's Your Job: These Are Your Rights," Washington, 1994.

21. Council of Chief State School Officers, *Using Youth Apprenticeship to Improve the Transition to Work* (Washington, 1994).

22. New York State Education Department, *A New Concept for Learning:*

Improving Public Elementary, Middle, and Secondary Education Results in the 1990s (Albany, N.Y., 1991).

23. Council of Chief State School Officers, *Using Youth Apprenticeship.*

24. Robert W. Glover and Alan Weisberg, *School-to-Work Transition in the U.S.: The Case of the Missing Social Partners* (College Park, Md.: Center for Learning and Competitiveness, 1994); and Richard Mendel, "The American School-to-Work Movement: A Background Paper for Policymakers and Foundation Officers," American Youth Policy Forum, Washington, 1994.

Chapter 6

PAUL OSTERMAN

Involving Employers in School-to-Work Programs

The 50 percent of young people who do not proceed to college directly from high school are poorly served by the education and training they receive. High schools fail to provide the skills the job market requires, and the transition from school to work is unstructured and haphazard. To ease the transition, school and work must be more closely coordinated. This could invigorate schools by reconstructing academic learning around occupational themes and would facilitate labor market entry by providing more formal pathways. A model for doing this is the German apprenticeship system, in which young people spend several days a week working in companies in structured training settings and the remaining time in school participating in a curriculum organized around and motivated by the work experience. At the end of their apprenticeship they receive both a degree and a certification of competency based on nationally recognized standards.

But the German system is more a reference point than a model for America; literal adoption is neither feasible nor desirable in this country. Nonetheless, virtually all current ideas call for substantial employer involvement in providing training or learning opportunities through job placements for young people while they are still in school. The intention is to create a new school-to-work transition system that would serve a substantial portion of American youth. During the 1992 presidential campaign Bill Clinton spoke ambitiously in these terms, and this objective presumably lies behind the 1994 School-to-Work Opportunities Act. But is employer participation likely at the intensity of commitment and the scale that are necessary?

There are reasons to be nervous about the answer. First there are the sheer numbers. If 25 percent of high school juniors and seniors eventually participate (thus reducing the forgotten half to the forgotten

Helpful suggestions were provided by Steve Hamilton, Richard Kazis, Lois Ann Porter, and Larry Rosenstock.

quarter), 1.5 million placements will be required each year. Currently, there are perhaps 1,000 slots in apprenticeship demonstration programs. One can broaden the concept of work-based education to include technical preparation institutions, career academies, and cooperative education, but at the cost of losing some of the program elements envisioned by advocates of the new initiative. Nonetheless, it is worth considering these other programs, which together enroll 500,000 young people. There is, however, also a problem of quality. Many of these slots, particularly those in cooperative education (which accounts for about 400,000 of the placements), are essentially after-school jobs and lack the structured learning envisioned for thorough-going programs.[1]

Beyond the numbers of jobs and employers required, there is little knowledge about what it takes to involve employers. Although many businesses have participated in particular training programs, few programs have included the elements envisioned in the 1994 legislation. Nor have there been systematic efforts to learn how to involve employers by testing alternative strategies and recording the results. The only real evidence is anecdotes from disparate demonstration programs. As a consequence, little can be said with certainty. This chapter, however, presents what information there is from the scattered sources and attempts to make the best judgments possible.

THE CONTEXT

What are the aspects of labor market structure that might shed light on the probability of extensive employer participation? First, in January 1995 some 31 percent of young people who were in high school worked, and 44 percent were in the workforce.[2] However, the overwhelming proportion worked in jobs that demanded few skills (table 1). The fact that they typically worked in "youth labor market jobs" suggests on the one hand that the jobs might be harnessed and relabeled as placements, but on the other that young people will have difficulty finding jobs or training slots with employers who are likely to provide much training.

The numbers should not be surprising. A great many young people churn through low-wage, low-skill jobs before settling down in their mid-twenties.[3] However, an important component of this pattern is the aversion of "good" employers to hiring what they consider turnover-

Table 1. Occupational and Industrial Distribution of Workers Aged 16–19 and 29–31
Percent

	Aged 16–19	Aged 29–31
Occupation		
Sales	10	6
Clerical	19	18
Laborer	11	5
Service	31	10
Other	29	61
Industry		
Wholesale and retail	44	17
Other	56	83

Source: Author's calculations from the National Longitudinal Survey of Youth.

prone youth. They prefer to hire employees in their mid- to late twenties who have a demonstrated commitment to work. In the British Youth Training Scheme, which on a very large scale sought to provide training jobs for recent school graduates and dropouts, 41 percent of the placements were in retail trade, although these jobs accounted for only 20 percent of the total jobs in the economy.[4]

The problem is compounded because U.S. employers do not seem to perceive a skill shortage, which would lead them to alter their attitudes. When the National Survey of Organizations asked employers whether recruiting qualified people was difficult, 40 percent said it was a minor problem and 45 percent said it was no problem at all.[5] A Harris survey conducted at the same time reported that 25 percent of employers said they faced a problem recruiting qualified high school graduates; only 15 percent had trouble finding skilled labor.[6]

Many newer tendencies in personnel practice also weigh against employer involvement. For example, a report by Mathematica Policy Research described a demonstration program in Chicago involving Sears and one in California involving Bank of America that were both cut short after the companies embarked on restructuring that entailed layoffs and hiring freezes.[7]

THE COSTS OF PARTICIPATING

Many employers, then, will not perceive that there are any substantial benefits from participating in work-based education programs, at least as viewed from the narrow perspective of their employment needs.

Perhaps, however, the costs of participation are sufficiently low that it is worthwhile. Fieldwork suggests otherwise. According to Mathematica Policy Research, employers "often reported that the cost of staff time for supervision or structured training is an even more serious obstacle to participating in youth apprenticeship programs than student wages."[8] This conclusion is supported by Dietmar Harhoff and Thomas Kane, who found that among larger German employers the annual costs per trainee net of the value of output was $9,381 in 1980; in smaller firms it was $5,991 (the estimates are in 1990 dollars).[9] In both cases wages were only half the costs; supervision and equipment accounted for the rest. The authors believe that these figures overstate the real costs to smaller businesses because training is integrated into production and off-line training is likely to occur in slack times. However, they believe the magnitude of cost is essentially correct for larger companies.

Estimates from American programs also support these conclusions. ProTech in Boston, one of the best known and most successful apprenticeship demonstration programs, places high school juniors and seniors into after-school and summer jobs in hospitals (the program has expanded to financial services and is entering environmental management and other areas). These students then pursue postsecondary education. According to one hospital, which has twenty-eight students, the total cost is $249,000, of which $90,000 is wages. This comes to $8,892 per student, including wages, and $5,678 excluding wages. These are gross costs. The hospitals believe that the students are productive and to an unknown extent the costs are offset by the value of their work. Nevertheless, in the short run it seems likely that the costs exceed the benefits.

The costs facing employers who participate in these programs are not limited to wages and training expenses. Students generally do not remain with the employers who trained them. Labor is highly mobile in the American market; in 1991, 28.8 percent of American workers had been with their employers for less than one year, compared with 12.8 percent of German workers.[10] The record of American vocational education is also weak in this regard: only 27 percent of vocational education students work in occupations related to their field of training.[11] Of course, one might argue that a well-designed school-to-work program will have better success, and this is certainly possible. But right now the outcome is speculative.

There are also intangible costs of participation. Perhaps the most important is the opposition of the adult labor force to the extensive use of cheap youth labor in a context of broad economic insecurity.

THE BENEFITS OF PARTICIPATING

Although the prospects for widespread employer participation seem bleak, I have yet to consider the possible benefits of participation. A significant percentage of employers believes that these benefits are real. A 1991 Louis Harris poll conducted at the headquarters of large corporations found that among those who were somewhat familiar or very familiar with new ideas for youth apprenticeship programs (42 percent of the respondents), 22 percent believed that their company's participation would help a great deal in obtaining a skilled labor force, and 48 percent believed that it would help somewhat.[12] (The survey did not clearly define the program elements involved; it simply referred to current discussions regarding apprenticeship programs. It is also important to understand that people in the headquarters of large corporations are often more accommodating and optimistic than are managers in the field.)

Participation may reinforce a sense of public-spiritedness and contributing to society. Many observers believe that these motivations lie behind many aspects of business participation in social projects. But it is difficult to believe that these laudable impulses can sustain a program of the magnitude that has been discussed. Businesses need to believe that participation is in their economic interest.

The most obvious self-interested motive is recruitment of a skilled labor force. Although the economy as a whole may not face a shortage of skilled employees specific sectors may indeed feel pressure. Again, ProTech is an example. The program began because Boston area hospitals were having problems finding good employees. To the extent that the immediate costs (cited earlier) of the students exceed the value of their production, they might be considered recruitment costs and amortized into the future. This is indeed the point of view adopted by the hospitals, although it is too soon to know how many of the program's students will in fact eventually work for the institutions that have participated in the program (a good sign is that of the first thirty-eight graduates of the program, twenty-eight are in health-related postsecondary programs).

Employers may also be concerned about the nature of the employees they are hiring. Banks have been hiring college graduates for even relatively unskilled positions such as tellers, but turnover has been unacceptable. The banks in the financial services version of ProTech appear motivated at least in part by an interest in finding more stable skilled workers. Equal employment opportunity concerns may also help participation. In the school-to-work programs at Cambridge Ridge High School, some employers seem to be participating because the programs provide qualified minority workers.

The experience of the British Youth Training Scheme bears out these observations. In a survey, 42 percent of participating employers said the program was attractive because it helped them screen potential hires.[13] But this advantage had a darker side. Employers apparently avoided providing training to program participants, preferring instead to screen the group, pull out the candidates they wanted, and place them into regular positions. Those not hired received no benefits from the program. By contrast, in ProTech, for example, employers participate in choosing which students will be admitted into the program and then hope that all participants will enter the health sector. Whether the abuse of screening would occur in a very large program, in which direct employer participation in early stages may not be feasible, remains an open question.

POLICY OPTIONS

The discussion thus far has implied that achieving a large number of employer placements is going to be very difficult. This is not to say that certain programs cannot be successful; excellent ones are in operation now, but the scale is still small. Replication is not simply a matter of doing many times what the few programs have done once. And it is more than likely that the demonstration programs have succeeded in part because they skimmed off the employers who for whatever reason were most likely to participate. To create far larger programs will be a major challenge. What are the policies that could increase the possibility of success?

As a first point it is important to recognize that the context within which policy operates may be more important than specific policies themselves. With respect to the school-to-work efforts, several contextual changes would dramatically increase chances of success. A substantially higher minimum wage combined with the option to pay participating youth less than the minimum would make these programs much more attractive to employers (this is in effect what occurs in Germany, with high negotiated minimum wages and lower apprenticeship wages). In addition, if it were much harder to lay off workers, the value of the kind of screening provided by apprenticeships would increase. And in a very tight labor market, low unemployment would induce skill shortages and make the school-to-work programs more attractive to upscale employers.

What these ideas have in common is that they involve decisions about the nature and course of the American economy and social system that extend well beyond the design of school-to-work programs. Various policymakers will, of course, have strong opinions about the merits and demerits of these tactics. But the important point for the present purpose is to recognize the considerable impact of background policies and structures that are rarely considered in the context of specific policy initiatives.

Beyond these broad considerations it may be helpful to classify policies into three groups. The first is policies designed to improve financial incentives facing employers. The second is ideas for making participation easier for companies. The third is ways of making it easier for program organizers to reach large numbers of willing employers.

Financial Incentives

One way to improve financial incentives is a training tax, which was proposed during the Clinton presidential campaign but then abandoned. All employers (presumably larger than a certain size—perhaps those with fifty or more employees) would be required to spend a certain percentage of their payroll on training or forfeit the unspent funds to the federal government. Obviously, many firms will want to avoid forfeiture and, if their training expenses are below the threshold, will increase spending. Providing placements and supervision for young people in apprenticeship or similar programs would certainly help employers meet the target, although this would presumably compete with training for incumbent adult workers.

Proponents of this idea cite its simplicity, but doubters note that in the European nations in which it has been implemented the grant-levy system, as it is called, discriminates against smaller businesses and invites what might charitably be termed creative accounting.[14] In any case, in the current environment it is the politics of tax policy rather than economic analysis that is the worst enemy of this idea.

Another means of improving participation is to provide firms with wage subsidies or tax credits in return for training young workers. Here U.S. companies do have some experience. Evaluations of the targeted-job tax credit, for example, suggest that net youth employment is indeed increased, but at the cost of considerable—perhaps 70 percent—leakage (that is, subsidization of youth who would otherwise be hired without assistance).[15] Subsidies of school-to-work programs could try to overcome this problem by clearly specifying the kinds of supervision and training companies would be expected to provide. If the rules were enforced, screening and training would probably improve. However, enforcement would be difficult. In current cooperative education programs, for example, written training plans are often not monitored or implemented.[16]

Beyond these problems is the question of whether subsidies are a good idea in the first place. Although advocates point to the prospect of inducing greater participation, opponents are concerned that unless the company perceives the young person as a real employee and a real member of the organization, the quality of the experience provided will be poor. In these circumstances the youth will be stigmatized, productive job assignments will not be established, and neither supervisors nor coworkers will take the youth seriously.

A final approach to financial incentives is for states and localities to link provision of learning positions to receipt of tax breaks in much the same way that some areas require that companies receiving breaks provide funds for housing and community development.

Making Participation Easier

The experience of demonstration programs suggests that the most important means of making employer participation easier is for programs to assign staff to act as intermediaries between the youth, the schools, and the employers. Employers find it frustrating to deal with schools (the typical characterization is that the two sides speak different languages) and as a result will often refuse to participate. Perhaps more seriously, the young people who enter the program will require considerable support to moderate their expectations, keep up their attendance, learn appropriate behavior, and maintain academic performance. Employers are typically concerned about these matters but hesitate to devote the time and take the inherent risks. Many of the demonstration programs have staff filling these intermediary roles, which they believe are essential.

In part these considerations are elements of program design and not policy, but policy arises when costs are considered. There is a strong case for requiring that the role of intermediary be built into program designs as a requirement for receiving support. But to do so invites significant additional costs. ProTech estimates that staff costs for these activities is about $2,000 a student (a considerable improvement from the first-year costs of more than $3,000 a student). Other programs have experienced similar costs. When this figure is multiplied by the number of students who may be expected to participate in a full-blown national program, resources become a major policy concern.

One way to avoid the high costs of the intermediary function is to embed the programs in the schools so that school staff are the intermediaries. (Many demonstration programs are now administered outside a formal school structure.) The question is whether this can be done effectively. There are successful examples: for example, the restructured vocational programs at Ridge High School and Latin High School in Cambridge, Massachusetts. But most schools do not have the necessary resources or may not be willing to reorganize existing activities to generate the resources. Typically, the ratio of students to guidance counselors is several hundred to one, yet proponents of the intermediary model believe that the ratio needs to be twenty-five or fifty to one. Beyond this, believing that the programs could be embedded quickly and smoothly bespeaks naive faith in the speed of educational reform. And, the problem of "different languages" is not solved because school personnel would be dealing directly with employers. At any rate, means of reducing costs should be weighed carefully and probably should be one focus of research resulting from the current initiatives.

Reports suggest that employers are also concerned about the initial investment required in developing training plans and standards. Here government and industry associations could be helpful in creating and disseminating standards and model programs.

Reaching Willing Employers

Policies must be able to help program organizers get commitments for large numbers of student placements without exhausting and inefficient effort. Many programs have had to trek from company to company, getting two positions here, ten there, and so on. The most successful strategy has been to work within industry clusters based on an assessment of local needs. Nonetheless, the going has been slow and tough.

There are perhaps two ways of making the process easier. The first is to follow what might be termed a community organizing strategy. In cities such as Boston and Louisville the business community has organized itself around issues of work and school. It is therefore possible to draw upon established contacts, experience of working together, and shared assumptions. Employers can be approached as a group. A worthwhile use of public funds would be to seed, encourage, or even require this kind of business organization in other communities. To some extent the planning process envisioned in the School-to-Work Opportunities Act can be conceived in these terms. Such a strategy could be boosted by a national campaign led by the president to encourage the business community to focus on work-based education matters.

A second strategy would be to recruit employers through intermediaries such as employer associations. This currently fashionable idea holds that associations are more credible in the eyes of their members than are schools or government agencies and can reach larger numbers of employers. Associations help make a case for the programs, which government agencies often have difficulty doing. For example, a number of demonstration programs have reported that employers discovered unexpected benefits from participation. The process of thinking through how to train young people led them to reconsider the training they provide for their regular employees. In turn this led to higher levels of training and productivity. This is a tale most convincingly told by one group of business people to another.

Although these ideas hold considerable merit, most associations are of the public relations or lobbying variety and do not engage in education and training.[17] There are, however, notable exceptions such as the National Tooling and Machine Association, which suggests that calling on associations has potential value.[18] Public funds could be used to provide incentives for them to build up the recruiting function and to create programs for involving their members in education and training issues. Among other tactics for encouraging associations, small grants could be provided to support "community audits" in which an association surveys its members about important education and training issues. Such an audit can naturally lead to deepening involvement in programs.

SOME FINAL THOUGHTS

Although individual training and education programs of high quality have been created and can certainly be replicated, it is very uncertain whether they can be established on a large scale. Where does that leave us? A useful place to begin is to think through what we care about most. One view is that training placements lead to skill acquisition and even credentialing and can directly ease the transition from high school into the workplace. Some programs such as ProTech want students to continue on to postsecondary education, but they still expect that their occupational experience while in high school will influence post-postsecondary education. These objectives clearly emphasize the quality of the work experience. The job needs to be real and to offer the acquisition of measurable and saleable skills. When a program such as ProTech can be created, young people's gains are impressive. But the chances of widespread program imitation seem unlikely.

An alternative way of understanding school-to-work programs is to interpret the work experience as a lever for reforming the school curriculum and for encouraging young people to continue on to postsecondary education regardless of the field they pursue. Acquiring vocational skills in high school then becomes less crucial. If this is taken as the goal, a much broader range of programs, including cooperative education, various job shadowing programs, technical preparation programs, and career academies, will become useful. Because this model asks less of the employer, it is much easier to think about the creative use of the youth labor market jobs, jobs many young people already have, in companies that have demonstrated their willingness to hire them. On a much smaller scale, it still is possible to design programs that are attractive to upscale employers who see training young workers as in their economic interest. However, most skills training will become the province of secondary institutions.

The idea of changing the goals of school-to-work programs will draw students, educators, parents, and employers into a discussion of school reform and financing policies for postsecondary education. In many respects this may be the most promising direction.

NOTES

1. Irene Lynn and Joan Wills, *School-to-Work Transition: Lessons on Recruiting and Sustaining Employer Involvement*, (Washington: Institute for Educational Leadership, 1994).

2. *Employment and Earnings* (February 1995), p. 24.

3. Paul Osterman, *Getting Started: The Youth Labor Market* (MIT Press, 1980).

4. Peter Cappelli, "British Lessons for School-to-Work Transition Policy in the U.S.," National Center on the Educational Quality of the Workforce, University of Pennsylvania, 1993, p. 14.

5. The National Survey of Organizations was conducted in 1991. Because the survey is based on the distribution of where people work, the answers are representative of all establishments, with firms weighted in proportion to the size of their employment.

6. Louis Harris and Associates, study 902062, August 1991. The Harris survey was conducted in 1991 among members of the Conference Board, which are the largest corporations in the United States.

7. Alan M. Hershey and Marsha K. Silverberg, "Employer Involvement in School-to-Work Transition Programs: What Can We Really Expect?" Mathematica Policy Research paper prepared for the Association of Public Policy Management, October 29, 1993.

8. Ibid., p. 8.

9. Dietmar Harhoff and Thomas Kane, "Financing Apprenticeship Training: Evidence from Germany," John F. Kennedy School of Government, Harvard University, October 1993.

10. Organization for Economic Cooperation and Development, "Enterprise Tenure and the Churning of the Country's Workforce," Paris, March 8, 1993, table 3.2.

11. Larry Rosenstock, "The Walls Come Down: The Overdue Reunification of Vocational and Academic Education," *Phi Delta Kappan* (February 1991), p. 434.

12. Louis Harris and Associates, study 902062, August 1991. Among these respondents, 36 percent said their companies were very likely to participate and 29 percent said they were somewhat likely.

13. Cappelli, "British Lessons for School-To-Work Transition," p. 15.

14. For a discussion see Paul Osterman and Rosemary Batt, "Employer-Centered Training Programs for International Competitiveness; Lessons from

State Programs," *Journal of Policy Analysis and Management,* vol. 12 (Summer 1993), pp. 456–77.

15. John Bishop, "Does the Target Jobs Tax Credit Create Jobs at Subsidized Firms?" *Industrial Relations,* vol. 32 (Fall 1993), pp. 289–306.

16. Lynn and Wills, *School-to-Work Transition.*

17. Patricia McNeil, "The Role of Industry Associations in School-to-Work Transitions," Manpower Demonstration Research Corporation, New York.

18. See Osterman and Batt, "Employer-Centered Training Programs."

Chapter 7

THOMAS BAILEY

Summary, Discussion, and Recommendations

Interest in school-to-work transition programs emerges from two concerns: that the workplace has changed, demanding new and different
skills, and that the schools have failed to live up to the challenge of teaching those skills. Analysts have been particularly critical of the education
received by young people who do not go on to college. To help remedy
the problem, they have created the school-to-work transition model,
which combines curricular and teaching reform with structured work-
based learning. Although very few programs include all the elements of
the model, several contain important components. These programs
include youth apprenticeship, cooperative education, high school academies, tech-prep, and reformed vocational education (see chapter 1 for
descriptions).

Many school-to-work proponents argue that the work-based component is crucial. The chance to experience a workplace, to learn in a setting
in which skills are used to accomplish something concrete, and to be
exposed to adults working in a variety of jobs has important cognitive,
motivational, and behavioral effects that cannot, they contend, be learned
in the classroom.

There was a consensus at the conference on school-to-work transition
programs held at the Brookings Institution that work-based learning has
many benefits, although some participants pointed out that there is still
little empirical evidence on the effects on learning or post-high-school
wages of the school-to-work model or the work-based component.
Participants disagreed on the extent to which the benefits of work-based
learning could be achieved in an appropriately designed school program
or school-based simulation and on the advantages and disadvantages of
paid and unpaid work placements.

One of the primary matters addressed during the discussion was
young people's attitudes toward work and what are often called job-

readiness skills. Several participants emphasized that employers complained about immaturity and the absence of a strong work ethic among the young, which is one reason why they are reluctant to take on interns and apprentices. Employers were also more interested in values, discipline, and general problem-solving skills than in specific vocational skills. School-to-work proponents argue that work-based education is particularly effective in teaching these types of attitudinal and generic skills.

INCENTIVES FOR EMPLOYER PARTICIPATION

Chapter 2 focuses on three motivations for employer participation: philanthropic, individual, and collective. Much of the participation, especially the more ambitious activity, is motivated by employers' commitment to improving their communities. These philanthropic motives have supported the development of a variety of models and pilot programs, but it seems unlikely they can support a nationwide program requiring intensive participation.

Participation in work-based education may be in the individual interest of some employers. Providing work placements can help them screen potential job applicants and often has some public relations value. But both benefits could probably be achieved with less intensive programs, perhaps no more ambitious than traditional cooperative education. Some proponents of school-to-work programs contend that employers participating in work-based education may enjoy unexpected benefits. Mentors or skilled workers who help train interns, for instance, may develop a new interest in training and technology. And participation can encourage employers to reassess the efficiency of their business operations. This is an attractive argument, but there is little evidence on how strong this effect is. Thus the discussion in chapter 2 is skeptical about the possibilities of an extensive system with significant employer participation based primarily on the individual interests of the companies in which students would be employed.

Joan Wills, director of the Center for Workforce Development, who conducted a survey of cooperative education programs (all with paid internships) and their participating employers, held perhaps the most optimistic perspective at the conference. Her survey responses showed that employers were satisfied with the quality of the co-op students and considered them productive employees. And although even large companies usually hired only a few students, the educators running the programs did not seem to have trouble finding enough placements.[1]

But the discussion at the conference was generally skeptical about the chances for significant growth of work-based education that depended primarily on the self-interest of individual employers. Harry Featherstone, president of a small metalworking company in Ohio, told a particularly discouraging story. His company is committed to training and innovation in the use of human resources. The employees are organized into self-managed teams responsible for their own volume and pace of production and paid according to their output. This is the type of company that would seem to understand the necessity for improving the education and skills of the next generation of workers. But the team members, Featherstone said, do not want young interns. They doubt their abilities, dislike their attitudes, and claim they would disrupt the pace of work and thereby decrease the compensation reserved for the adult workers.

Conference participants who had organized work-based education programs often look to public or nonprofit organizations for job placements. Bob Yurasits, the principal of New York Technical Coop High School, which runs a school-based enterprise program, finds projects around New York, such as renovating substandard buildings, and organizes the work experience for his students. There is no wage cost to the employer. But Yurasits only works with public and nonprofit organizations.

Xavier Del Buono, president of Workforce LA, a coalition of schools, community colleges, and businesses in Los Angeles organized in the late 1980s to improve the linkage between education, training, and work, has found work placements for thousands of young people. Workforce LA depends on the public sector and the quasi-public health care industry. Del Buono commented that there are at least three barriers to greater private sector participation. Many businesses provide little training for their workers and are therefore not inclined to help train young interns. Many employers are also reluctant to hire teenagers. Finally, even if jobs in the private sector could be found, many would not offer a high-quality educational experience.

I argue in chapter 2 that the collective interests of a group of employers in the same industry (or perhaps employing large numbers of workers in the same occupation) might be a stronger basis than individual interests for larger work-based education programs. Youth apprenticeship pilot projects have been concentrated in such industries as metalworking and health care, where employers very much need new workers and have been able, especially in health care, to work together to develop their workforce.

But there are problems with programs that depend on collective interests. They will be weakened if proponents emphasize, as many do, that school-to-work programs should open doors to higher education at least as much as to immediate employment. If students go on to higher education rather than take a job in the industry, the programs may not strengthen the industry's labor force. A collective approach also needs some institutional structure through which it can be organized and articulated.

The discussion on these subjects led to another one of the main themes, emphasized by several participants of the conference: the importance of employer organizations. Workforce LA provides an interesting example of the function of industry organizations. The coalition's first program involved work placements in public sector jobs. Students were given some instruction to prepare them for work, but the program was not integrated into school curricula. Although the coalition now has a variety of programs, the one that Del Buono believes works best involves industry-specific consortia that decide how their industries should relate to school-to-work efforts. The most successful of these are in health care and transportation; many of the work placements in transportation are related to the extensive construction of Los Angeles's rail system.

LESSONS FROM THE EUROPEAN EXPERIENCE

European educational models have been influential in the development of the school-to-work programs in the United States. Margaret Vickers's chapter focuses on differences in employer participation in Germany, Sweden, and the United Kingdom. In the German system employers hire 60 percent of each youth cohort as apprentices in structured programs that are coordinated with academic instruction one day a week. The Swedish system requires that vocational students spend 15 percent of their time in unpaid internships, but the system is primarily school based. Employers take a significant part in establishing the curriculum in their industry areas. Work-based education in the United Kingdom is organized around the system of national vocational qualifications. Industry groups are instrumental in setting the NVQs, and employers teach and assess student performance of the skills required for the certificate.

Most of the discussion at the conference focused on Germany, which is not surprising because Americans know much more about the German system than the programs in other European countries, and it has had the strongest influence here. Several participants reaffirmed the strengths of the German system for producing a highly skilled workforce. Berndt Söhngen, head of the Department of Education and Training at AG Bayer, emphasized that apprenticeship at Bayer is intended to "equip young people with the widest possible sense of the world of work," not just the skills needed for their current jobs. The initial training is designed to minimize the need for retraining when conditions change. Exposure to a real working environment, he contended, taught crucial interpersonal and communication skills as well as specialist skills.

Participants also confirmed Vickers's point that the German system was based on a unique institutional, cultural, and legal tradition. They emphasized the importance of a culture that supports employer involvement in training as well as government involvement in the workplace and a close employer-employee relationship. Compulsory paid membership for employers in the employer organizations (chambers), the strength and influence of unions, and the involvement of the government in regulating the quality of the training on the job all contribute to the success of the program.

But the German system is experiencing problems, a situation particularly important given the extent that U.S. policymakers have looked to Germany for guidance. In some sectors there are shortages of training places. In the past the shortages have been associated with demographic fluctuations such as the baby boom. But perhaps a greater problem now, emphasized by Vickers and other conference participants, is declining interest among young Germans in apprenticeships, especially in industrial sectors. Peter Van den Dool, head of Policy Analysis of the Directorate for Vocational and Adult Education of the Dutch Ministry of Education, commented that more and more students consider academic education the route to better jobs and more money. Stuart Rosenfeld, president of Regional Technology Strategies, stated that according to a 1994 report there were 100,000 unfilled apprenticeship slots in Germany.[2]

Berndt Söhngen noted that although this number is probably accurate, sectors and occupations vary. For example, in Germany as a whole there are only 100 applicants for every 115 sales and administration apprenticeships. Filling apprenticeships for blue-collar occupations, especially when shift work is involved, is also often difficult. Söhngen pointed out that despite Bayer's good reputation as a trainer, applications for the 1,700 new training contracts every year dropped from 13,000 at the end of the 1980s to 6,000 in 1994, and of those 6,000 applicants, 60 percent were interested in administrative and commercial professions. Bayer does not get enough qualified applicants to fill apprenticeships for skilled production technicians, despite the occupation's relatively high pay. Nevertheless, both Söhngen and Van den Dool were enthusiastic about apprenticeship programs and believed that current problems with applicants did not necessarily imply a movement away from a work-based system. Measures should, however, be taken to increase young people's esteem for vocational education and blue-collar work.

In chapter 3 Vickers comments that given the need for a particular institutional structure to support an ambitious work-based system, the Swedish experience might have more lessons for the United States than the German system. Sweden has recently consolidated its system so that hundreds of occupational lines for students in upper-secondary schools were reduced to fourteen broad clusters. About half of all students are enrolled in these clusters, while the other half are in one of two academic clusters. Employer organizations at the national level are intensively involved in developing curricula for the clusters. In the United States, Oregon has developed a similar system based on a small number of occupational categories. But as Vickers points out, although this model has attractive characteristics, there are no definitive empirical assessments of its effectiveness relative to other models.

The system in the United Kingdom may have important lessons because the United States is also developing industry-based skills standards that reformers consider crucial to the success of the school-to-work strategy. But according to Vickers, skills standards will not have a significant effect on work-based education if the training capacity within the participating firms is inadequate. Program operators in the United Kingdom have indeed found that the capacity in many British firms is limited. Vickers contends that the most successful NVQs have been those in Scotland in which the training is provided by so-called further education colleges rather than by the employers.

HOW SCHOOLS MUST CHANGE

In chapter 5 Robert Poczik argues that schools must develop new methods to be able to recruit employers and work with them effectively.[3] But even if enough employers can be found, school-to-work programs will not succeed if they are simply appendages to traditionally structured schools. The programs require significant in-school reforms, and there are many barriers to those reforms. For example, despite years of work and the encouragement of the 1990 amendments to the Carl D. Perkins Vocational Education Act of 1984, few schools have developed the curricula and teaching methods appropriate for integrating academic and vocational education.

To be able to work effectively with employers in developing a comprehensive school-to-work system, Poczik states that school administrators and teachers must be committed to the success of the innovations. The appropriate training of teachers and counselors is also crucial. Parents and students must be convinced that work-based education opens up rather than limits subsequent opportunities. It is also crucial that schools include employers in all steps of the planning and development of a work-based system and make certain there are adequate numbers of well-prepared mentors at work sites. Schools will also have to figure out how to assess and give credit for work-based learning. Finally, educators must integrate innovations in work-based education with other school reform movements.

Structural barriers stand in the way of many school reforms, Poczik comments. Because many students are already working and are engaged in many other activities, the extra time needed for work-based education often discourages their participation. The flexibility required to schedule work-based education comes into conflict with the structured, bureaucratic nature of most high schools. There is a persistent tendency in education to undervalue less academically inclined students and to reward students who succeed with classroom instruction. A successful work-based education system would require a change in this type of attitude. School reformers too often adopt an innovation before previous reforms have been in place long enough to have a significant influence on teaching and learning. Economic conditions may discourage schools from taking on the necessary commitments. Finally, in many urban and rural areas, high rates of business failures, unemployment, and poverty make it difficult for students to find jobs.

The conference participants described some of the steps that schools must take to work successfully with employers. George Chambliss, the career education coordinator of Middle College High School in New York City, said students are required to do three unpaid internships during their four years in the school. To accommodate the internships, the school has reorganized its schedule and faculty responsibilities. The classroom periods are all seventy minutes rather than the more typical forty-five or fifty minutes—and the school uses three twelve-week cycles rather than two semesters. The internships each last twelve weeks, and the students are on the job from noon to 4:00 p.m. four days a week. They take two classes in the morning during the internships. Because of the reorganized schedule and a focus on academic classes while in school, students get the same amount of academic preparation as students in other schools despite the time on the job.

The interaction between teachers and the employers and work sites is crucial to the success of the Middle College program. Before each internship, students take job preparation courses. The first course focuses on job finding and appropriate behavior at work. The second addresses the role of the student in the family, community, and work group. The third concentrates on decisionmaking and planning for the future. The teachers who conduct these classes are responsible for monitoring the internship and working with employers. They also lead a once-a-week seminar during the internships in which students can discuss their experience and integrate what they are learning on the job with school activities and their lives in general.

Middle College places 1,000 students a year with about 165 employers. These placements have been steadily developed since the late 1970s, and Chambliss reported that it is not too difficult to find placements for all the students, especially because some students find their own internships. Chambliss stated that he has become a "twenty-four-hour job development machine," using every opportunity to ask employers if they will take an intern.

The program has had more success with small businesses than large. Internships in small companies are usually more varied because the division of labor is less well developed. Chambliss has also found that sustaining a relationship between the school and a workplace depends on the interactions between the teacher or teachers and a particular employer. Establishing relationships with personnel departments of large companies has been much less successful, which is another reason Middle College internships tended to be with small employers. Chambliss and other Middle College staff are enthusiastic about the internship program. Informal follow-up studies conducted internally have suggested that students pass 25 percent more of their courses after their internships.

The Middle College experience gives some idea of the magnitude of the changes necessary to mount an internship program. School staff have reorganized the schedule and semester structure, designed a curriculum to prepare students for their internships and integrate school and workplace experiences, and developed extensive personal relationships with a large number of employers. And these internships are short-term, unpaid placements; they are much less ambitious than those envisioned by many proposals for work-based learning. Finally, the program is designed to promote personal development and career choice and awareness more than teach specific job skills.

POLICY RECOMMENDATIONS AND ALTERNATIVE ROLES FOR EMPLOYERS

Public policy to encourage employer participation attempts to provide stronger incentives, reduce barriers that stand in the way of the incentives employers do have, and, especially with respect to collective incentives, provide the means through which employers' collective interests might be articulated. Paul Osterman's chapter on public policy addresses five broad themes. He first discusses the influence of context (the national labor market and the institutional and legal structure) on participation, then describes three classes of policies or practices to promote involvement. Finally he urges policymakers to take a broad view of what constitutes workplace learning and incorporate it into comprehensive educational reform. The remaining discussion in this chapter is organized around these five broad themes.

Broader Contextual Conditions

Osterman argues that because cultural, institutional, and legal characteristics influence the viability of a work-based education system, basic changes in these characteristics would create an environment in which employers would have greater motivation to participate. A stronger tradition of hiring and training young people would help, although this is not something that can be created by policy. But potentially effective policies include higher minimum wages with exceptions for registered apprentices, financial or regulatory restrictions on layoffs, mandatory dues-paying membership in employer organizations, an activist macroeconomic policy to promote employment growth and dampen economic downturns, more monitoring and regulation of learning and training on the job, and regulation of hiring practices to favor applicants with particular types of certification. These measures would involve significantly greater government regulations and control of the economy, so whatever their merits, chances of enacting the policies in the current antiregulatory climate seem slim.

One conference participant, Anthony Sarmiento, assistant director of the Department of Education of the AFL-CIO, advocated providing incentives for incumbent workers as well as employers. These workers would be expected to provide much of the mentoring and instruction and could cause serious problems for any program if they believed apprentices or interns were taking jobs or training opportunities away from adult workers. Stronger unionization would help provide incumbents with a vehicle for organized participation in planning and implementing work-based learning efforts. Sarmiento also urged that school-to-work efforts be incorporated into the many existing union-related training programs and other education reforms.

The federal government might create a more favorable environment for participation by supporting research on work-based education. Employers would be more likely to become involved if there were convincing measures of the educational benefits of work-based learning, and if they had a better idea about how much participation would cost them, what benefits they might derive from it, and which practices were most effective.

Federal and state governments can also recognize and publicize the contributions of particular companies, which could also encourage involvement. Marc Tucker, president of the National Center on Education and the Economy, pointed out that the United Kingdom has established an Investors in People award to recognize firms that have established innovative training and development programs and that have integrated the programs into their business strategies. This prestigious award is similar to the Baldridge award in the United States.

Individual Financial Incentives

Various financial incentives for employer participation in school-to-work programs have been proposed, but their potential effectiveness is debatable. Subsidies could, for example, support employers who might have participated without the subsidy. Wage subsidies have sometimes been found to reduce the employment chances of workers whose pay is subsidized. Apparently, some employers believe that the subsidy signals a problem with the worker. Programs in which employers are required either to participate or to pay a tax—so-called pay-or-play programs—would encourage "creative accounting." In any case, as Osterman points out, the politics of tax policy rather than the economics of subsidies is the greatest enemy of financial incentives. The Clinton administration abandoned a training tax proposal even before taking office. And given the current mood of Congress in the 1990s, new taxes or subsidies, as well as new regulatory measures, would seem to have little chance.

Perhaps because of political realities, there was little discussion at the conference of fiscal or regulatory measures to promote employer participation. Marc Tucker agreed that incentives to individual companies, such as pay-or-play schemes—referred to as grant-levy in Europe—would not be effective, but experience in other countries indicated that some government support for employer organizations might be cost-effective and would avoid some of the drawbacks of individual subsidies or taxes. He suggested that an Investors in People award might be linked to a limited subsidy. This approach would also encourage companies with high-quality jobs to participate, because those with few such jobs would not be able to win the award.

What Schools Can Do to Facilitate Employer Participation

At least for the time being, significant fiscal and regulatory measures to promote employer involvement seem unlikely, and federal resources to promote the School-to-Work Opportunities Act are not likely to grow. Even the current act, passed when legislators were much more sympathetic to federally led education reform, contains no specific incentives or regulatory reforms designed to promote employer involvement. But there are measures that schools or program operators can take.

Osterman emphasizes the importance of having counselors or other personnel act as intermediaries between schools and employers, a role prominent, for example, in the internship program at Middle College High School. Effective counselors can build personal relationships with employers, help students adjust to the work site, and help employers solve problems associated with the employment of interns.

Other steps can also build employer trust, ease anxiety and misconceptions about participation, remove associated problems and barriers, and improve the potential benefits. One review of school-to-work programs has stated that a successful strategy to recruit employers involved four broad measures: clarifying the expected roles and responsibilities of participating employers, targeting those most likely to participate, approaching them in ways that promote trust, and maintaining and deepening participation.[4] Other suggestions include helping employers understand or avoid potential legal problems associated with child labor laws.[5] Because there is some evidence that participation strengthens commitment, the key to program growth may be recruitment with appropriate support into modest programs. Once employers are on board, they begin to lose many of their misconceptions and see that young interns can make a contribution.

Some employers report that cooperative or internship programs help them screen potential recruits. Schools can strengthen this function by choosing appropriate students to send to particular jobs, providing information about the students to employers, and working closely with employers during the period of the work placement.[6]

As Osterman comments, cost is one drawback to these school-based efforts. The counseling function in one pilot program costs $2,000 a student. Providing additional services to employers to encourage involvement would add to that cost. But costs could drop as programs expand and achieve economies of scale. The work-based component may also replace other aspects of an educational program and save money elsewhere. In any case additional costs would have to be evaluated against the benefits. Unfortunately, there are no definitive measures of the benefits.

Better recruitment and screening of students also has drawbacks. The effort could lead to selecting only the most attractive for internships, which creates equity problems and controverts the inclusive philosophy of the school-to-work approach.

But despite these costs and drawbacks, schools can take steps to strengthen their efforts to involve employers. The measures may not be able to reach many, but the whole school-to-work idea is still too new for us to have a strong sense of their limitations.

The Role of Employer Associations

Employer associations can also do much to promote participation. As Osterman points out, they offer the opportunity for program operators to reach employers without having to develop work placements employer by employer, although operators will still have to develop individual relationships with employers. Associations may also be more effective in convincing employers of unexpected benefits from participation or that hiring an intern or apprentice may not have so many costs and drawbacks after all. The associations may even have staff to help develop work-based education pedagogy and curricula. In some industries, employers may have a collective interest in developing the skills of their potential workforce, but that interest can be articulated only through a collective organization.

Although in the United States most employer associations have traditionally focused on lobbying, not training, they have shown an interest in recent years in working with schools to strengthen young people's skills, and many have become involved with efforts to develop industry-based skills standards. One of the participants at the conference, Cheryl Fields Tyler, was the director of workforce excellence of the American Electronics Association, which is involved with a skill standards pilot project and a variety of training-related efforts. The federal government has also traditionally sponsored industry consortia for research and development. For example, the Cooperative Research Act of 1984 led to more than 400 consortia for cooperative research efforts within particular industries or sectors.

At the conference, Marc Tucker reported on an Australian program based on industry or occupationally oriented group training corporations. These not-for-profit corporations recruit employers and manage the administrative work associated with work placements. In this arrangement the apprenticeship or internship (and the legal liability) is with the corporation, not the employer. The corporations work with schools, oversee the content of the work placements, and work with on-site mentors. The employer pays the students but is spared the cost and time required to oversee and coordinate the work-based component of the program. Group training corporations are subsidized by the Australian government, which Tucker believes avoids direct payments to employers and supports only the necessary overhead of the strategy, something that is particularly onerous for small employers.

Promoting the involvement of employer associations is probably a good activity for state governments to pursue. Even if subsidies are not forthcoming from state legislatures, governors' offices might be effective in working with appropriate associations. And some of the funds sent to the states under the School-to-Work Opportunities Act could be put to use for strengthening the involvement of employer associations.

Although associations may enable schools to reach a large number of employers, public agencies may be similarly helpful. Robert Poczik, director of workforce preparation, New York State Education Department, reported that New York State was working toward setting up agencies (perhaps through contractors) that would have a centralized listing of participating employers (including those willing to participate in other public employment and training programs such as the Job Training Partnership Act or work-welfare programs). This listing would help prevent too many education or training programs from contacting the same employers.

Employer Participation and Broader Education Reform

Two subjects have dominated this book and the discussion at the conference. The first is the incentives employers have for participation in school-to-work programs, especially by providing work placements. Much of the policy discussion has focused on measures to strengthen those incentives by enhancing the benefits, lowering the costs of involvement, or increasing the costs of noninvolvement. The second theme has been the trade-off between the intensity and spread of employer involvement. Most of the authors and conference participants agreed that fully integrated apprenticeships or high-quality internships closely related to classroom learning with a clear occupational focus may produce great benefits for students but will be difficult to achieve on a large scale.

Still, there are many ways employers might be useful if a broader view is taken of what constitutes a valuable contribution. David Stern's chapter outlines alternatives at three levels of participation. The first involves only a commitment of resources such as equipment or money, which characterizes many of the existing school-business partnerships. The second requires some commitment of time on the part of the employer or the employer's workers: counseling students, providing instruction in classes and opportunities for field trips, and giving advice about curricula, instruction, and assessment. The third and most demanding level requires changes in the internal operations of the company, although even within this level some practices are more demanding than others. These include providing job shadowing and unpaid internship opportunities, offering placements or internships for teachers, recognizing new skills standards, and encouraging student attendance and performance.

Vickers's chapter illustrates the different levels of employer involvement in different countries. In Sweden, employers were intensively involved in the development and assessment of curriculum, but mostly through employer associations. In the United Kingdom employers were involved in both developing skills standards and teaching and assessing those skills. They have had more success as advisors than as trainers. Germany is an example of the most intensive form of employer involvement.

Work-based learning is one of the most distinctive features of the school-to-work model, and as a result work placements have attracted a great deal of attention. But interest in school-to-work strategies emerges from a general belief in the need for broad education reform. Internships and other work-based experience can be important in that reform if they are an integral part of it. Indeed, one of the potential pitfalls of initiating work-based education is that its difficulties may distract educators from needed changes within the schools. Moreover, once the variety of roles that employers could assume is considered, it becomes possible to view their participation as a contribution to general education reform rather than primarily as a source of work placements.

With the help of employers, schools can make considerable progress themselves in introducing changes that incorporate many advantages of work-based education. Reforms such as the integration of academic and vocational education or a more project-based approach to teaching and learning appear to have potential. And in-school programs such as school-based enterprise (discussed in Stern's chapter) can also contribute. As Poczik and Osterman as well as some conference participants argued, it is important to link the school-to-work movement more closely to other reform initiatives. Some participants expressed a concern that unless the school-to-work strategy is viewed comprehensively, it could deteriorate into a marginal, second-class program of unstructured work experience for students who do not appear to be college material.

With these cautions in mind, structured work-based learning still appears to have great potential, and it is too early to know the practical limits to its expansion. Like any policy, there are costs in money, time, and energy, associated with development. Governor John McKernan of Maine, who attended the conference, had chosen the development of his state's apprenticeship program as one of the two or three priorities of his governorship. Time and political capital spent on recruiting employers is less available for other initiatives.

Of course, there are benefits to be balanced against these costs, although little is known about the balance. So it is useful to think of work-based education along a continuum of intensity. At some point the additional costs required to increase the intensity of a work-based education component may outweigh the additional benefits. Ultimately, the experiences of hundreds of thousands of students in job shadowing programs or short, unpaid internships may be more valuable than those of a few thousand in sophisticated apprenticeships. The School-to-Work Opportunities Act and the many related state initiatives have now set in motion hundreds of pilot projects that, if carried out systematically, can answer many of these questions. Only with the knowledge developed through this experience will this promising educational strategy be incorporated into the core of the country's educational system.

NOTES

1. The results of this survey are reported in Irene Lynn and Joan Wills, *School Lessons, Work Lessons: Recruiting and Sustaining Employer Involvement in School-to-Work Programs* (Washington: Institute for Educational Leadership, 1994).

2. See Industrial Research and Development Advisory Committee of the European Union, "Quality and Relevance: The Challenge to European Education," Paris, 1994, p. 36.

3. Poczik's chapter was commissioned after the conference and is based partly on his experience leading the New York State school-to-work implementation program.

4. Susan Goldberger, Richard Kazis, and Mary Kathleen O'Flanagan, *Learning Through Work: Designing Quality Worksite Learning for High School Students* (New York: Manpower Demonstration Research Corporation, 1994).

5. Lynn and Wills, *School Lessons, Work Lessons.*

6. Robert Zemsky, "What Employers Want: Employer Perspectives on Youth, the Youth Labor Market, and Prospects for a National System of Youth Apprenticeships," Working Paper 22, National Center on the Educational Quality of the Workforce, University of Pennsylvania, 1994.

Authors and Discussants
with their affiliations at the time of the conference

Thomas R. Bailey
Institute on Education and the
   Economy, Columbia University

George Chambliss
New York City Board of Education

Xavier Del Buono
Workforce LA

Harry E. Featherstone
Will-Burt Company

Jack Jennings
Committee on Education and Labor,
   U.S. House of Representatives

John R. McKernan, Jr.
Governor, State of Maine

Paul Osterman
Sloan School of Management,
   Massachusetts Institute of
   Technology

Robert Poczik
State Education Department, The
   University of the State of New York

Stuart Rosenfeld
Regional Technology Strategies

Anthony Sarmiento
AFL-CIO

Berndt Söhngen
Bayer AG

David Stern
Organisation for Coopération et
   Développment Économicques

Marc S. Tucker
The National Center on Education and
   the Economy

Cheryl Fields Tyler
American Electronics Association

Peter van den Dool
The Netherlands Ministry of Education
   and Science

Margaret Vickers
Technical Education Research Centers
   (TERC)

Joan Wills
Institute for Educational Leadership

Robert Yurasits
New York City Technical Coop High
   School